The Rise of the Cyber Women: Volume 2

Compiled by

Lisa Ventura

Copyright Notice

Contents

Introduction by Tyler Cohen Wood

It is such an honor to write the introduction for a book celebrating 16 courageous women who embarked on incredible cyber journeys. And even though each woman's journey is unique, a major theme stands out in each story—the obstacles and challenges each one of them had to face to overcome adversity. Each one of them had a point in which they had to find the courage and strength to conquer obstacles and become the thought leaders they are today.

My story too is about finding my strength and finding my voice. I worked hard, learned to succeed in a male dominated industry and thought I was strong, until I had to face the most challenging obstacle I'd ever have to face. And little did I know that it would be my 22-year career in cybersecurity and the skills and lessons I learned along the way that in turn would literally save my life and gave me the opportunity to save many other people. Here is how it happened.

I started my cybersecurity career in the late 1990s, early 2000s. Strangely, it was my name that helped opened doors in my early career. Each time I applied for a job and showed up for the interview, the interviewer would always seem shocked when I walked in the door. They all thought I would be a man. This is how I landed a job with a large web hosting company, working overnights in the SOC. Back then, we only had Windows NT and Sun Solaris machines. I was the only person on duty in the SOC overnight so I began to learn everything I could about UNIX and Linux. I was obsessed and couldn't get enough. Eventually, I became good at the job and was the first one on the SOC to get promoted. I thought that my teammates would be happy for me, and some of them were, but most were not. They made comments about how I only got the promotion because I was a woman, not because I was a quick learner and obsessively studied books and proactively found ways to make our monitoring tools work better. It was hard enough to try to fit in with the guys, but this made me more of an outcast. I was young and hadn't encountered this before and it made me feel as if I had to overcompensate to make up for it. Even though I knew it was wrong and unfair, I said nothing and let it fester for the early years of my career.

In 2004, I moved to Washington D.C. because I wanted to learn how do digital forensics to help federal law enforcement. It was my UNIX and Linux knowledge that landed me the job working for the US Department of Defense Cybercrime Center. The interview was terrifying because it was a panel of ten people asking me forensics-specific questions. At the time, I didn't have the answers. The only interview questions I was able to answer very well were UNIX or Linux related. Lucky for me, they desperately needed a UNIX/Linux person, and I was her. I loved that job. I learned quickly and it turns out I was good at digital forensics. I also really loved the people I worked with. They were a pretty even mix of men and women and I found strength in bonding with the other techie women, but also in bonding with the techie guys. However, this job was different because I can't remember a single time while I was at the DoD Cybercrime Center where I felt as if I was treated differently because I was a woman. In fact, we were a strong team and we all helped each other because our mission was so demanding. I realized that I was very good at finding ways to develop out-of-the-box solutions to some of the most complex cases. I remember one case that involved a sexual assault on a young woman that had been digitally recorded on a cell phone. We didn't have smartphones back then and phones were much more basic technology. No matter what forensic tools I used, I could not find the video on the phone. I got assistance from other forensic examiners, but we still couldn't find the video. This case was one of the toughest that I had worked on and I knew that if were unable to retrieve the video, the suspects would walk free. I believe that there is a solution to every problem and didn't want to give up. Just as I was about to admit defeat, I had an idea. Back then, phones would receive updates and perform backups via a computer. I searched for backups of the phone on a suspect's computer and sure enough, I was able to retrieve the video. It was the understanding that came out of this case, that every problem, no matter how complex, has a solution that would turn out to be my saving grace.

Even though I had a two hour commute each way to and from work, I didn't care because I felt like I was part of something bigger and I loved being able to help people. Without question, the Cybercrime Center was one of my favorite jobs. There were hard times too. Some of the major crimes cases against children were really tough but, again, we all worked together as a team to make sure that the victims got closure, regardless of the nature of the case. I did not want to leave the Cybercrime Center, but the commute finally got me. I had the opportunity to go to US Defense Intelligence Agency in a leadership role.

The DIA is where my career really started to take off. This role would force me to dig deep into my ability to develop complex unusual solutions that would keep the US special forces safe when operating in high-risk areas. This is where I first had to learn to stand up for myself and for our division. Again, I was very lucky because I worked with many brilliant women and we stuck together and helped each other out. I worked extremely hard and proved my worth time and time again by developing many successful complex cyber solutions. I was eventually promoted to Deputy Division Chief and was one of the highest-ranking women in the Science and Technology directorate.

Everything changed in 2014 when I wrote *Catching the Catfishers*, a book to teach parents and kids how to keep themselves safe online. Because of this book, I started to do many media interviews and speaking engagements. DIA had very stringent policies about media interviews and writing books. It quickly became apparent that I had to decide whether to continue doing media and speaking engagements or stay in the intelligence community. It was a really hard decision, but I chose to leave the agency and go into the private sector. This opened the door to being able to do media and cybersecurity keynote presentations all over the world. I loved that I was able to help groups of people make cybersecurity something empowering and even fun. I felt as if I was making a difference in the world and helping to demystify cybersecurity. I started to feel confident and happy. But something started to feel off. And this is where the second part of my story begins, where my strength would be tested in ways that I never could have imagined.

In early 2018, I got sick. It started off as what was thought to be a food born infection. I ended up in the ER and was told I had colitis. I just assumed that it would be a quick fix. But things didn't get better, they got worse. And it began to progress from there. My symptoms were horrible. I will never forget the first GI doctor I saw for my stomach issues. He told me that even though the blood test results showed abnormalities, I just had a food borne infection and it would clear up on its own. He then told me that I seemed "stressed" and that stress was making it worse than it was. He was dismissive and made me feel as though I was doing something wrong. Most of the doctors that I saw truly wanted to help, but unfortunately, this dismissiveness and disbelief would be a trend as I was shuttled from doctor to doctor for the next 2 years, as I got sicker and sicker without knowing what was wrong.

I found myself stuck in an endless loop of being shuffled back and forth between specialists. specialist A would send me to specialist B who would send me right back to specialist B.

This is how I learned about specialty siloing. Many of the doctors in my journey wanted to help and wanted to collaborate with my other doctors, but they didn't have a way to do it. I quickly realized that the onus is on the patient to obtain their medical records and test results, review them, consolidate them, and try to determine what records were pertinent to helping the doctors help me. This is where my cybersecurity training kicked in. First off, I was taught to investigate complex issues. I realized that there were not enough hours in a day for a doctor or anyone else to review and put relevant test results into a chronology and a meaningful summary so they can be quickly assessed by the doctor. I devised a method to consolidate all results to try to give the doctors a quick summary instead of giving them 100s of records. It was the information in this chart that caught a serious mineral deficiency that without correction would have been life threatening. But we still didn't know the whole story and I was getting sicker.

Through it all, I had to pretend as if I was healthy. I felt ashamed that I was sick. I had had a successful career and a thriving life, and I was rapidly becoming a shell of a person. I continued working and doing speaking engagements, but it was really hard to fake being healthy. I started reading medical papers to enhance my knowledge so that I could help make sure the doctors had everything they needed. But I kept hitting the specialty silo wall. And I was only partially diagnosed. I felt as if my identity was slowly being taken from me and that I was losing my own sense of personal dignity. I started to lose faith in myself and I began to lose hope. And I was still trying to hide that I was sick. I was so afraid that if anyone found out, I would never get a job again. I drew on the strength that I'd built through my many years cyber experience and being able to thrive in an obstacle strewn professional environment. So, I fought through the physical and emotional suffering and got to work.

I created the MyConnectedHealth concept. I knew that I needed a team of healthcare professionals, a patient crowd and the best of technology working together on my case, with me (the patient) at the center. In late 2019 I finally found the right team of doctors and felt as if we were getting somewhere. And then came COVID-19, and the world changed overnight. Almost overnight, telehealth became mainstream. I knew that I had to make MyConnectedHealth a reality because I had to help.

In May 2020 while developing manual AI logic statements for MyConnectedHealth, using my own medical data and test results, I plugged one seemingly insignificant set of test results into the script and it returned a specific diagnosis in a completely different lane than where we'd been looking for years. I looked up the condition, a rare autoimmune disorder, and it explained my past and present symptoms to a T. I immediately checked with my doctor who agreed that it was likely, and a specialty blood test confirmed the diagnosis that the system indicated. The prognosis for me isn't great, but now I know what I have and that makes all the difference. The system has the ability to help the millions of other people who, like me, suffer from a chronic, hard to diagnose or rare disease and who need help. I know a cure is out there for me and for so many others and we will find it.

It's an exciting time for healthcare technology and the cyber industry in general. As a woman in cyber, and as a patient and patient advocate, I draw on strength built up over a career and a life of both challenges and triumphs and look forward to more of both. I feel blessed to have learned so much from my cybersecurity career and from the strong women and men that have been there through it all. Each of our stories is unique, yet the theme of strength, perseverance, and a refusal to give up has made each of us the strong women that we are today, and I am honored to be a part of it.

Disclaimer

The chapters in this book have been submitted by those featured. As such the writing style of each chapter has been kept as far as possible particularly with regard to culture, language, terminology and how the chapters are constructed. The chapters are a mix of first person and third person accounts, and American spellings have been retained in some of them where appropriate.

Each chapter is unique to the writer and the Editor did not want to change the essence of the chapters submitted, although the book has been proofread by the Editor and a third party for clarity.

All chapters have been approved and signed off by the individual contributors.

Acknowledgements and Thanks

My sincere thanks go to everyone included in this book for taking the time to write and submit their chapters for inclusion. I also express my thanks to all the women in cyber security all over the world who we have interacted with in the course of compiling this book and for their insights, hints, tips and more to help others who are considering a career in the cyber security industry. You have all inspired me to do more, be better and to achieve more. Thanks also go to Gill Tolley of AssignIt2Me for proofreading this book, and to my husband Russell Ventura for his unwavering support.

Finally, I would like to extend my sincere thanks to everyone in the Infosec community on social media, particularly on Twitter and LinkedIn, who I have got to know and who have supported me with this project. You know who you all are.

Lisa Ventura

Editor: The Rise of the Cyber Women: Volume 2

Chapter 1

Name: Lianne Potter

Job Title: Information Security Transformation Manager

Company: Covéa Digital and Technically Speaking Leeds

Location: Leeds, UK

"You know why they've hired a load of women this time round don't you?
So, we [the company] look good on diversity stats…"

This was my first day at my first job in tech.

The year before this moment flashed before me; all those hours of studying, those times I neglected my family and friends, the hobbies I shelved, the get-togethers I declined, and the financial hit in taking an entry-level role. These were the sacrifices that I had made in leaping from being a 'non-technical' person to landing my first technical job at the age of 30 as a software developer and cyber security evangelist.

It would be all worth it, I told myself.

A tech career is where I wanted to be. It was my vocation. A year into my re-training, I had done nothing but live-and-breathe the industry. I was on the frontier of an exciting new chapter in my life; I did not know where it would take me but, I knew the adventure would be worth the sacrifices I had made in getting here.

My excitement at starting my first job in tech was instantly tainted when that sexist comment hit my ears. I was at my desk no more than five minutes, when I overheard a colleague positing his theory as to why this latest round of recruitment featured more women. I was not supposed to overhear this; in fact, they did not even know I was there as I sat there obscured by two large monitors.

I continued to listen, burning with rage, feeling the lump in my throat expand, hot heat stinging behind my eyes, and willing myself not to cry (my unfortunate default when I am furious).

"How dare they?! After everything I've done to get here!" I thought to myself. I had every right to be here - and it was not because of my gender.

I had put in the work, done the assessment days, the interviews, the tests - the same as everyone else who wanted to work here, male and female. I had earned my place on merit, not affirmative action.

Before embarking on a tech career, I did my research. And something did keep coming up time and time again: the tech industry is not diverse, discrimination was a problem, some organisations have a prevalent 'Bro culture', and more than half of women leave the industry by the mid-point of their career (more than double the rate of men).

But surely this would not apply to me? What I had read must either be an exaggeration or outliers rather than par for the course in this industry, I reassured myself.

After all, all my closest friends are men. I am a gamer who likes mindlessly blowing away zombies. Six of my top ten films are testosterone-laden 80s action movies (with at least three of them featuring Arnold Schwarzenegger!). As a tomboy, there was no way that I could be at the receiving end of toxic masculinity. How naive I was!

It is no fun raising a HR issue on your first day - *I can tell you that much.*

Reaching for the Stars

Becoming a software developer and then later pivoting again to my dream job in cyber security is something I still have to pinch myself over.

I grew up in a poor part of Leeds where the consensus was, if you made it past high school, then you were 'doing well.'

As a child, my friends' ambitions were to have children as soon as possible - school was just a holding place until those ambitions were realised. They were the product of generations of joblessness. Our teachers did little to encourage us to study hard or suggest that there might be more out there that the world could offer us.

I often felt like an outsider growing up. I was an avid bookworm. As a small child, I would spend hours carefully studying 'The Usborne Children's Encyclopedia'. Carefully, I would turn the pages and make notes in my book listing all the things I wanted to see with my own eyes, the places I wanted to go, and all the jobs I wanted to do: artist, author, historian, doctor, scientist and the one I would come back to time and again, astronaut.

I was ten when I begged my parents to decorate my room like a space-scape. The wallpaper was of the solar system, consisting of a repeating pattern of planets and stars that went on forever, including a deliciously large Saturn, which I would trace with my fingers as I lay in bed. It was paired with a cheerful border of spaceships and floating cosmonauts cutting through this galaxy covering my four walls and no space themed bedroom would be complete without the obligatory glow-in-the-dark ceiling stars. Once the lights were out, I would stare up and picture myself working at NASA, floating around in the International Space Station, and posing proudly in my spacesuit.

I was lucky to have supportive parents who encouraged me not to follow the crowd. They wanted better for me, even if they did not quite know how to get me there. Even from that young age, every decision felt as if it was a path *never* trodden, let alone least taken! So, what does one do for advice at age ten? You ask a teacher - they know everything after all (ten-year-old logic)!

I remember bounding up to my primary school teacher and with precocious earnestness and telling her:

"I want to be an astronaut when I grow up!"

There was a pause that seemed like an eternity. She furrowed her brows and shook her head: 'Girls aren't good enough at science and maths; so, you can't be an astronaut. Be an English teacher instead."

Very deflated, I gave a heavy, wordless nod in agreement.

If I was drawn to the weightlessness of zero gravity as an astronaut, the denouncement of my dreams, brought me crashing to earth with a bump. Taking her word as gospel, I resigned myself to a restricted future, and with that, gone were my dreams of becoming an astronaut.

A Crash Down to Earth

Although I did well in my studies by the end of high school, I never pushed myself in maths and science. I never stopped being fascinated by science, but I packaged it away as something that I could not pursue very seriously. My teacher's explanation that girls were not naturally any good at those subjects became a self-fulfilling prophecy and I actively avoided those subjects, choosing to focus on English and Art instead.

When I obtained my degree in English Literature, I was the first person on both sides of my family to go to University. It was hailed as my ticket to bigger and better things, a degree in those days still carried with it a promise of a good job and stability. But a few months before I was due to graduate it seemed like the whole world was imploding on itself as the financial markets took a nosedive. The news was full of talks of the worst recession since the depression, joblessness was on the rise, and all those graduate training jobs that I had my eye on disappeared. I had to find a job, any job, quick.

I took the first job I could, a low paying job in a hotel's administrative pool - a job that was quite far from the promises that obtaining a university education previously held.

The difficulty with roles like administration is that it can be challenging to move out of that role and do something else. People struggle to see past a job title, no matter how hard you try.

I knew I could do more, but it would take me nearly ten years before I got a chance to prove it.

The Digital Divide

After many years in various administration roles, I began working for a local charity. I quickly flew up the ranks and finally felt like I was getting somewhere in my career when I was promoted to the project lead for a new initiative for which we had recently won funding. The initiative was to get the local people out of destitution. It was a daunting task but one I could not wait to support.

We had no idea what circumstances people would come through our doors with but, as word quickly got out that we were open for business, we were booked weeks in advance with new clients.

It was an emotionally draining job with people sent to see us from local credit unions, council offices, job centres, social workers, women's shelters, homeless centres, and drug support units. Their lives were chaotic, their backstories heart breaking, and their situation dire.

Many would walk through our doors with less than ten pounds to their name or, they would be hungry not having eaten in days. Our job was to give our clients stability and get them out of destitution. The people coming into our service would tell me things about their life that would keep me awake at night, making me thankful for the roof over my head. Despite the emotional strain, I adored that job and found the work challenging but incredibly rewarding.

Early into the project, we noticed that the majority of our time was spent accessing services online on behalf of our clients. We would often hear from our clients that they had gone to the jobcentre to sign on for benefits only to be told it was all done online now. They would tell the centre that they did not have access, nor did they know how to use a computer. The response they got was to go to the library and learn how to use a computer. Our clients balked at this. Many of our clients had low literacy or severe anxiety (or both). So, faced with the prospect of going to the library, many of them were very intimidated by this proposition. But it was not just for claiming benefits that we saw this digital barrier, which I would later learn is called the 'digital divide'. We saw its impact in all aspects of life: housing, mental health referrals, education, even things like getting the best price for gas and electricity would have a significant impact on our clients' lives. It seemed the world was geared towards a client base who had the means and the experience to navigate a digital world.

Our work went beyond helping people out of destitution by completing online forms for them. It became a means of gathering testimonials and examples of when important services were penalising and socially disadvantaged people due to their ability (or inability) to access digital services online. Services needed by the most vulnerable people were being redesigned based on the assumption that everyone has access to the internet and possesses the skills (or the inclination) to use it. We became advocates for our clients. Our service would bring this inequality between the info-haves and the info-have-nots to the attention of the people in power and those who created the services without considering the end-user.

I became enthralled with the subject of 'tech for good' and the pitfalls of creating digital products and services for the most vulnerable in society, without consulting them or their ability to access such things in the first place. It spurred me on to research the digital divide rmally through a Masters in Anthropology via distance learning. While studying, I would aydream about a career that would enable me to do tech for good, utilising what I knew out the realities of digital access.

A Christmas Redundancy and a New Year Challenge

he third sector is not an industry for long-term job security and despite the impact we had n our clients, our project was subject to a funding cut, resulting in redundancies, including y own, two days before Christmas in 2017. Although the timing could have been better, and was sad to be leaving a job I adored, I saw redundancy as one heck of a career motivator!

ot relishing the prospect of another decade in the admin pool, my redundancy gave me the rive to do something completely different. It felt like fate when just as I received my final otice at the charity, I serendipitously saw an advert online from one of the largest tech firms Leeds. It was advertising a recruitment drive to get more women into technical roles, ecifically, software development, a job I barely knew what it was.

s I felt those familiar feelings of doubt like I had done back when my teacher said I could ot be an astronaut, I wondered, 'Could I be a software developer? Didn't I need to be good at ience and maths to be one?' I had no reference point to guide me this time. At that point, y only experience of software development was what I had seen in films (and 90% of that nowledge was based on the Matrix - not the most accessible reference point to my future areer!).

ut I thought at the very least I should see what the tech industry had to offer, and this pportunity came with the promise of free training so why not give it ago? To my delight, I as invited to their open day.

could barely contain my excitement when I arrived. It looked positively space-age to me! It as like my childhood imaginings of NASA, with screens everywhere, vibrant people busy at eir laptops creating amazing things; all with the addition of an on-site hipster coffee bar, iill-out rooms, and beanbags. Certainly not the cash strapped, make-do, and mend ivironment I had just come from.

he open day began with the company telling us why they needed more women to increase e diversity of thought, ideas, and experience. To create better products and services and eet the needs and lifestyles of their customers and represent them. I lapped this up! This as exactly why I wanted to get into tech, to help democratise it. They followed up with me hands-on coding exercises which I picked up quickly. As the day drew to a close, they xplained that the demand for their scheme was more than they anticipated (300 women had pplied for 18 spaces) and, if I were successful, I would hear from them. I left their offices on loud nine, convinced this industry was for me, even a technical role!

s the weeks went by I checked my emails constantly to see if I was one of the lucky 18. nd then one day the long-awaited email arrived...

Dear Lianne, thank you for coming to our open day, due to a large amount of interest in this cheme, we regret to inform you...."

I was gutted but, unlike my childhood rejection, I thought to myself, 'Their loss', and set out on the task of teaching myself how to code. I had tasted the possibilities of a tech career and there was no stopping me.

I knew that if I was serious about a tech career, then I needed to take it seriously. I made learning how to code my full-time job while I was in between jobs, and so began my many months glued to Freecodecamp.org, Code Academy, YouTube, and going to every single tech meetup in Leeds I could so I could join this exciting industry.

Naturally Paranoid? How about Cyber Security?

It was while I was spending every evening at tech meetups that I happened upon a talk about cyber security delivered by the NHS. As soon as the first speaker started talking I knew I was hooked!

Did I have strong attention to detail? Check!

Did I have a protective side to me? Check!

Was I paranoid about getting hacked...like all the time? BIG CHECK!

Should I be looking at cyber security instead of being a developer? I began to ask myself. As much as I loved to code, I could not help but wonder if after all those years in the admin-pool and keeping pin-point sharp at spotting mistakes, that perhaps, my skills would be more suited to this part of the industry. To this day, I still think the best people for cyber security roles are ex-PAs and administrators! After the talk, I plucked up the courage to speak to the presenters to see how I could break into the industry. As much as the presenters were encouraging, it seemed like it was much harder to get into this sector than it was to be an unconventionally trained software developer. Backed up with copious amounts of Google research, yes, it did seem that cyber security was driven towards degrees and certificates more so than software development.

I decided then, the best way into cyber security was to carry on with my developer training but alongside it, learn as much as I could about cyber security too. My theory was, if I could make inroads with software development, then I could pivot to cyber security from the inside - if not, I would still be in tech - win-win. It turns out this was the right move and being a developer who loved security made me a very rare beast in this industry. But re-training for two careers simultaneously was exhausting. I would get so frustrated at my lack of free time, and the compromises I had to make in place of yet more sessions in front of a computer screen. I came close more than once to throwing in the towel and giving up altogether.

But every time I was on the brink of giving up, I would be drawn back in by my tech tribe.

Tech Tribe Assemble

Learning to code on my own was all great fun with me making cat apps and card games until it was not fun anymore. When I hit the dreaded learning curve, the concepts I was learning got harder and harder, and I ended up spending more time gritting my teeth at broken code than revelling in the glory of a well-executed function. I would curse my sausage hands for every missed semicolon or spend hours correcting syntax errors from unforgiving languages. Coding became a chore. I would sit at my computer either screaming or crying. I started to think that this was all a mistake. That I had wasted my time, neglected my family, and for what? If I got stuck I had no-one to ask for help and I would lose days on a broken line of code.

That was until I found my tech tribe.

I had spent so much time in isolation on my retraining journey that I needed to ask someone:

"Is it supposed to be this hard?"

"Am I kidding myself that I can retrain for a career in tech in my 30s?"

"What does 'job ready' look like?"

"Am I hyperventilating right now?!"

I knew carrying on in this way would lead to burnout and then I would end up giving up and all those months of teaching myself to code and cyber security principles. It would have all been for nothing.

After a quick Google, I found out that Leeds has quite the buoyant tech community, catering for nearly every flavour of tech that you could want. I had plenty to choose from and every night in the city was another chance to learn about the industry.

I found my tech tribe. These were people who loved to geek-out on tech. Having gone through the same highs and lows of learning their craft, they welcomed me, not in spite of my newness to the industry, but because of my newness. People wanted to be my mentor because they knew what it was like to start on this tech journey. I had never come across an industry that has been so geared to seeing its peers succeed.

It made me stronger during the tough times, especially when I began spending more time focusing on cyber security which seemed like such an allusive industry and a bigger gamble to aim for.

Save Lives, Protect the NHS...

After five months of barely broken screen time, I saw a vacancy advertising a role on a graduate training scheme for software developers. Although I knew I wanted to be in cyber security, I was also quite aware that that particular sector was not going to open to a person with a background like mine. So, I stuck with my plan: Get a job in tech, any job, learn all I can and then pivot to cyber security from there.

The job was for a governmental organisation, for its digital arm. I was a little apprehensive because, at aged 30, I felt a little too old to be considered a graduate. But I knew I had to start from somewhere and hoped they would give me a chance to prove myself.

It was during my interview that I realised how far I had come. I told them about all the hours I spent learning how to code and my love for cyber security, my dedication to re-training, all the meetup groups I had joined, the conferences I attended out of my own pocket, how I wanted to help people with tech and how much I had fallen in love with all things tech.

I was proud of myself in the interview. I was confident I had just as much right to be there as any computer science degree.

The interviewers must have thought so too, and I was offered the graduate role - which I instantly accepted.

First Day HR Woes, or just another day at the office?

We are now back to where we started - on my first day in tech, raising a HR issue for a sexist comment.

I would like to say that it was an isolated incident that got resolved quickly...I would like to say that.

Unfortunately, quite a lot of my tech career has been marred by things that bristles me.

Like every time I have gone to a cyber security conference, I have been asked if I work in the marketing department. Or at another conference when I overheard one of the vendors say that only a few years ago, the only women who would attend these conferences would be 'promo girls in bikinis serving beers' and 'isn't a shame that the 'golden age' of cyber security conferences was now over?' (this is not an exaggeration; I really did hear this!).

Or the time, when I finally got into my first cyber ops role and had a boss that refused to say 'hello' to me in the morning and utterly ignored me. The team passwords for shared licences were made up of female body parts. The time when I was given a book for secret Santa called: 'How to succeed without hurting men's feelings.' Or all the countless times I have been ignored at meetings or had my ideas dismissed and then regurgitated by a male voice and then accepted as if it was their idea.

In this industry, I am constantly reminded of my gender, which for someone who never really defined herself by gender, has been one of the hardest things to adapt to.

It could have gone a different way on that first day in tech. I could have kept quiet, internalized their words, doubted myself and my abilities. Perhaps, had it been my first job out of university, or, if I was a bit younger, I might have done that. But I took the choice to call out that behaviour on my first day. I used the hurt and anger I felt to raise awareness about the need for diversity in tech. It spurred me on to become an advocate and a public speaker on career re-trainers, and non-traditional tech backgrounds. So, in a way, I am grateful to that colleague who ruined my first day in tech. Without them, I might not have done the thing I am most proud of in my career: helped other people get into the industry.

Was Cyber Security everything I wanted it to be?

Cyber security is a very tough industry to crack. The days are long, the threats are unrelenting, and it can sometimes feel like you are that New York cop from those 70s movies where they keep saying: 'It's a warzone out there, man!' You can often feel like you are not even scraping the surface of the threats out there. But despite its flaws, there are very few industries where you feel like a bona fide superhero (even if your superpower is stopping people from clicking on phishing emails). When you avert a crisis or fix a mess, or educate someone on the dangers, there is no feeling like it. Despite the struggles, there have been some wonderful moments and true allies.

While it might not be space travel, the virtual world to me, is just as interesting and vast a place to be engulfed in. I am grateful I work in an industry where I have no choice but to keep reaching for those stars, from the safety of my keyboard rather than the space shuttle.

And you may ask yourself, well, how did I get here?

It has been nearly four years since I started my journey; I am still getting used to referring to myself as a cyber security manager.

The tech industry has presented me with so many opportunities that I would have never had. It has enabled me to set up code clubs teaching non-technical staff how to code. I founded my own health-tech company aimed at helping women go through menopause. I have become a public speaker and a tech activist fighting for digital inclusion. I have won several tech awards and, I have strived to be a role model for other women in tech.

Joining the cyber security industry changed my life; it can change yours too.

Here are some of my tips to help you get there:

- **Be dedicated to your learning.** When I first started re-training for a technical role, I devoted all my free time to it. No video games, no Netflix, even my allotment got neglected. This can be hard to keep up if you are working too or have other commitments, but you need to set time aside to learn your chosen technical skill every day. If you want to progress fast, you need to put the hours in. When it comes to friends and family members, make sure they are aware of your goals right from the start so they can support you and keep you on track (rather than make you feel guilty when you turn down their invitations). Join initiatives like 100 days of code if you struggle to keep focused.

- **Do your research and find the tech skill that is right for you.** Look for topics that you enjoy first and foremost but keep in mind what career path you will be interested in later down the line. It is hard to stick to something if it does not interest you, but it is even harder to stay motivated when you realise it is a waste of time.

- **You will never know everything about your chosen field.** Learning the basics is easy; becoming a master is hard. Try not to beat yourself up when things get tough. You will never know everything there is to know about the topic you are learning, but every day you will learn something new. Take pride in how far you have come, not how much you lack.

- **Find your tech tribe**. Find a group where you feel supported in your learning, where you can talk tech, learn new things, and make great industry contacts.

- **If you do not know something, do not pretend you do.** People are not generally very good at admitting that they do not know something. Do not assume people know what level you are at, and do not be afraid to ask for clarification. I have yet to come across anyone in this industry who was not happy to explain a concept when asked.

- **Be willing to take a step back in your career to go forward in the future.** The same day I was offered my first tech job, I was offered a promotion from my then-current employer which would have led to a significant salary increase. I had to make a choice: take the promotion and stop my tech ambitions, or take a pay cut and get a junior role doing something I loved. A "career change" is a temporary "career sacrifice" and you need to take a short-term risk before you see a long-term reward. I was lucky that I was financially able to make that decision. The next few years might be a bit lean on the salary front, but remember, tech is one of the most well-paid industries so it should not be for long!

- **Your non-tech skills are just as important as your tech skills.** If you are re-training, shout about your non-technical skills. Employers are recognising that technical skills can be taught, but soft skills are more innate. So, if you give killer presentations or are great at motivating a team, then make sure you let these skills shine just as much as your tech skills.

Finally, if you see someone new to the industry struggling, be kind, share knowledge, and remember we are all still learners.

Wherever you are on your journey, remember George Eliot once said:

"It is never too late to be what you might have been".

I would like to thank the following people on my tech journey:

Sean Sapsted, Simon Dyson, Simon Langley, Natasha Sayce-Zelem, Sarah Tulip

and of course, my loving husband, James Lester

Chapter 2

Name: Andrea Manning

Job Title: Founder & CEO

Company Name: CyberPie

Location: Galway, Ireland

Contact: amanningpro@gmail.com   **+353 89 429 7806**

"Since the men being the Historians, they seldom condescend to record the great and good Actions of Women; and when they take notice of them, 'tis with this wise Remark,
That such women acted above their sex.
By which one must suppose they wou'd have their Readers understand,
That they were not Women who did those Great Actions,
but that they were Men in Petticoats!"
Mart Astell, The Christian Religion, 1705

Credit: Unquiet Women, Max Adams

Women in Cyber Security are not Men in Petticoats!

How far have we come some three hundred years later? When women excel do we still run the risk of being 'Men in Petticoats'? Cyber security is an industry where women are still in the minority. As we strive to create a gender balance, we must push ahead as exceptional cyber security professionals and be seen this way regardless of our gender. Through the telling of our stories and journeys that brought us here, we can inspire and encourage others to join us. There is a seat for everyone at the table. The most effective way to enact change is representation.

Today I am a cyber security entrepreneur building a startup to give the microbusiness sector a piece of the cyber security pie. Whilst I'm your classic linear thinker, ironically, the path that got me here was by no means linear. And I certainly don't fit the mould of a typical cyber security industry professional. I'm a 52-year-old single mother who recently graduated university for the first time.

I had a privileged upbringing in South Africa and a great feminist for a mother. We were brought up to believe we could be anything or do anything, we had good schooling and opportunities yet the only girls that went to university were those that wanted to become teachers. I chose to go off to Hotel School and worked in the hospitality sector. At 23 I made the bold decision to head to London. I left without so much as a backward glance, my life packed up into a small blue suitcase and £300 in my pocket. Even in 1991 this was not a lot of money. London was everything it should be and more. I worked hard, partied hard, and held many positions. They ranged from an events manager for a Fawlty Towers-esque hotel in London to selling conference space at an infamous stately home. A short stint in the City followed and finally a twist of fate and unusual circumstance meant I landed up running a very successful removals company. I lived in the moment, I never said no to an opportunity, and never once considered the risks of anything I did. Miraculously I somehow survived, and thrived, through two decades of the high life. And then at 37 I fell pregnant and my job title became Single Mother. It was the best thing that ever happened to me and I never looked back.

Responsible for a child now, it was time to grow up and after a time I moved to the west coast of Ireland to make a better life for my daughter. I never gave a thought to my own needs but looking back, it was I who reaped the rewards. I toughed out the 2010 recession and scraped a living together by baking and setting up a market stall. A chance conversation with a fellow mum put me on the path to doing an access course at University. Earning a degree had always been unfinished business. I needed to prove to myself what I was capable of and that I deserved a seat at the 'clever table'. True to form, I said yes then figured out the details afterwards. If I'd known what was involved, including the maths, I would have run a mile. Taking some sage advice from one of the current students, I tackled it by looking at it on a semester-by-semester basis. Anything is possible if you only have to survive 12 weeks. So, there I was signed up for a full-time 4-year degree in Business Information Systems whilst juggling a full-time job. There was a lot more maths, some programming, data analysis and even Chinese. Finally, it was my gateway into all things technology. I loved it. Sitting next to 18-year-olds who had mums younger than me had its moments, group projects drove me demented but every day I learnt more. More about myself, more about the world, and more about what I was good at. If anyone who reads this even has a vague inkling of returning to college, all I can say is do it! It's one of the most rewarding experiences of my life and I cried happy tears the day I stood up in my black gown and cap and collected my first-class honours degree.

I made lifelong friends along the way and gained a whole new understanding of a generation who indeed will grow up in very different circumstances to the ones we did. They are a generation compelled to excel because they see they have no choice but to achieve. With this comes a maelstrom of anxiety, expectations that often can't be met, and a very unfair, unlevel playing field. Owning a home, having a job, having a pension are no longer givens. There's also no room to just be average; a luxury my generation took for granted.

All the while the common thread running through each job or career, I embarked on was my love of technology and an innate curiosity about how it all worked and how to leverage it. From the early hotel computer systems to visiting the IT department, located in the basement of course, of the Barbican Centre to have a go on the Internet. I was one of the first to build a website for my business moving us away from the Yellow Pages model. And of course, my degree was grounded in technology. I have always been an early adopter and love the fact that with technology the answer is always yes - all you need to do is figure out how. My mother is 84 and still upgrades to the new iPhone as soon as it comes when it's out. She's a whiz at setting it up and a very competent troubleshooter. Perhaps it's hereditary?

Fast forward - so now I'm a graduate with a great degree that's in demand, an abundance of soft skills so necessary for the tech world and years of experience in marketing and business. Bring on the dream job. Crickets….. nothing. My CV was not linear, it didn't show a clear career path, indeed it confused the humans and the algorithms. On the one hand I was very experienced, on the other I was a graduate with no experience. I was also 50. Couple that with a bit of disguised sexism and I would be offered PR, Marketing and Sales jobs when in fact I was applying for a technical role. Was it because I was 'chatty, and good with people'? I would guess that had I been male perhaps those associations might not have been made. Age, nor sex, should never define your possibilities, and after a good deal of soul searching and analysis, I came to see being a 'jack of all trades', or generalist as its now called, was indeed my superpower and not my failing. Whilst there is a move to recognising the benefits of hiring a generalist, the traditional hiring model and CV algorithm will still look for a single profession. Very few of us that are of an age can say we've stuck to Infosec - it didn't exist and wasn't a career option even 10 years ago. Good candidates are falling through the cracks.

The driving force behind my next decision was that no one had the right to put me on the scrapheap when, potentially, I was barely halfway through my life. Everything was pointing towards setting up my own business. Now I no longer had to be a square peg trying to fit into a round hole and it felt exhilarating. Forever more I would get to be a square peg and never have to apologise for it.
Here was my chance to be the change I wanted to see. A chance to build a business and create opportunities for others like me. Redefine the traditional definition of success, and challenge at what age it should happen.

My work helping SMEs get to grips with GDPR was the ideal starting point and the perfect opportunity to use every one of my skills; problem solving, simplifying the complex, understanding how tech platforms work, and communication of course. My GDPR work then opened the doors to cyber security - something I'd been teaching myself and finding myself drawn into. GDPR is not sexy. Selling its benefits and getting buy-in is a hard task. My innate positivity and optimism meant I was good at this. I made a point of finding the nuggets that win my clients over and helped them to see the underlying 'why'. Cutting through the jargon and the complex, it was my job to make it seem easy. Using my own experience of never doing anything unless I could understand why it was necessary, I sold the benefits of GDPR and how to use it to gain customer trust. I used my persuasive skills to show that GDPR can be used as a marketing tool and the benefits gained came from the process of doing it. But there was another area that was even more successful - security awareness. Helping business owners to put security in place, and indeed change some dubious practices was where it all began to sing. I soon realised cyber security was the gateway to GDPR for my clients. A way to get them onboard and embrace the change required. The stories about Russian gangs showing off in their Lamborghinis paid for by cybercrime, or true-life examples of invoice fraud, or simple hacks like turning off Bluetooth, brought the messages I had to deliver come to life. They were the most powerful way of instigating real lasting change that would make a fundamental difference to a small business. My very varied career history began to pay off. It meant I understood the trials of business and the issues business owners have to navigate and could recommend solutions that were practical to implement.

As an industry we still have much to learn when it comes to the delivery of our message. Scare tactics have much the same result as anti-smoking adverts: it's too much to deal with, so you change the channel. FUD (fear, uncertainty, and doubt) is not the way to go. Rather, being able to empathise, and then offer solutions that were relevant and practical is my winning formula. Break it down into small manageable tasks and it no longer seems so overwhelming. If you leave a client with a list of twenty security recommendations, what are the chances they will enact them? Ask them to do just one thing, such as install a password manager, help them install it and you've achieved far more. They say, 'teach a man to fish and he'll never go hungry'. Much the same with cyber security - empower the user with knowledge and resources and they'll be in a good position to take ownership of their security instead of holding thumbs and hoping the worst never happens.

The Infosec community is a treasure trove of resources and knowledge. Twitter can be one of the best starting points for anyone starting out. Ignore the petty stuff and seek out the knowledge. There's a lot out there and it's freely and generously given if you want it.

I see myself as a curator. I'm a voracious consumer of content online. There's a great acronym JFGI which pretty much means just $%*! google it. You'll be surprised how many people don't. Information overwhelm is the curse of the internet and as a result finding the information you need, and no more, is easier said than done.

Nothing is complicated, sometimes it's just explained badly. This applies to our own learning and to the information we need to share with others. As an industry we're no different to many other industries when it comes to gatekeeping. Have you ever told your GP that you googled your symptoms? Watch the shutters come down. Gatekeeping is a natural instinct to protect your domain. Like every other industry, gatekeeping is rife within cyber security. There's a good deal of mansplaining too. Unfortunately, there are those who set out to make it seem more complex than it needs to be, and only the domain of a select few. This gatekeeping will do us no favours. Furthermore, the very people we seek to protect and educate - our clients and users of the technology - are just regular human beings. They're living regular lives juggling priorities and resources and cyber security isn't their top priority. If we can't communicate with them in their language, and win them over, all the technology in the world won't prevent a cyber-attack. 90% of data breaches are down to human error. If we were to create a cyber security charter, the first commitment would be to keep cyber security human.

I'd like to hope that as cyber security careers become more mainstream, and there is a great deal of work being done in this space, that we don't look at the soft skill roles as a little bit 'second-class'. I have a good base knowledge of the technical side of security and huge respect for those working in this area. There are so many roles within the industry, and none should be seen to be more elite than others. Every role is a valid one and has its part to play. I've been fortunate to work on a few cyber security conversion programs and the students are always surprised to realise there are roles that are not purely technical. I've seen many an eye light up when they realise there are many paths that are open to them. Sadly, not enough of these roles are advertised or on offer. The more role models we start to see, the more we can create lasting change in this area.

Always make security awareness training personal. I learnt this when I needed to create a scenario that explained how GDPR benefited the individual and protected their rights. Using the example of a customer loyalty scheme, and the organisation sharing details about how much wine and beer one purchased with the insurance company brought home how vulnerable each and every one of us are. This was far more effective than drilling down into the intricacies of Article 27 or 44! One of my first security presentations was to a group of safari guides. A group of men who work in the field taking extremely high-worth clients on exotic safaris across Africa, coordinating private aircraft in the middle of the Masai Mara and generally doing the Indiana Jones thing. I had to find a way to engage them from the outset as they too are at risk of cybercrime, be it invoice fraud, identity theft or their client's travel arrangements falling into the wrong hands. Showing them the details, one could discover from a boarding pass barcode got their attention straight away. The sessions lasted twice as long as planned because the questions kept coming. They were engaged and wanted to make changes to protect their livelihoods.

Working with startups I always share the author Tim Ferris's 11 'Reasons Not to Become Famous'. How at risk he and his family are now that so much of their private life is public. The larger your audience the more you're at risk for extortion, stalking, death threats and desperation messages. Everything you do online and offline is a potential security risk. For example, he writes *"The more visible you are, the more people will attempt to impersonate you or your employees. This could be to hack a website, access a bank account, get a SSN, or otherwise. Companies or fly-by-night entrepreneurs will also use your name and face to sell everything from web services and e-books to shady info products and penis pills (sadly, all real examples). This is something that my lawyers deal with on a weekly basis. It's non-stop. For both reputational and liability reasons, it's important to track and guard against much of this."* Sobering advice but it brings the message home.

Working with small e-commerce traders I show them how easy it is to install malware on their website or how to protect their Facebook Ads account from being taken over. All these examples are personal and relevant. At heart we're all selfish — if it's not about me, I'm not really interested.

The best advice I was given was to find something that sizzles your bacon! Cyber security does that for me. It's a combination of technology, psychology, intrigue, communication, people and above there's little chance of reaching the boredom threshold. It's ever changing with new learning and developments daily. Being an inherently curious person has served me well. I will always seek out more information and I love the treasure hunt aspect of a problem. I'm also a rule breaker. If you're in cyber security, do you recognise these traits in yourself?

My mission now is to make cyber security accessible to everyone — not just the big corporate organisations that have dedicated security awareness training programs. What about the microbusiness sector? Does an accountant or physiotherapist take themselves off for a day of security awareness training? I think not. But are they vulnerable to things like CEO fraud, or having their email account taken over? Very much so. Sadly, the stats show us that 60% of small businesses will go out of business within 6 months of falling victim to a cybercrime. Also, it would be very short-sighted to think that this sector isn't part of the larger supply chain. That saying 'A rising tide lifts all the boats' can apply here too. In cyber security it's no longer okay to just make sure your organisation is okay. So now I've found my niche and my mission going forward.

My entrepreneurial venture is CyberPie. An all-in-one cyber security platform that will empower the small business owner to build security into their business, one bite at a time. And all without the FUD! The small business is an easy target. It typically has fewer protections in place and little or no monitoring. Cybercriminals don't choose small businesses — rather their defences are just easier to break through. And the results can be devastating. After the many hours spent hours down the cyber security rabbit hole learning about criminal gangs with Lamborghinis, dark web shopping lists and off-the-shelf ransomware, I wanted to find a way to bring this to a sector that doesn't typically have access to security awareness training. We learn by telling stories and these stories have the power to educate and inform but in an engaging way! I also realised that the cyber security community is a treasure trove of advice, simple fixes, and workarounds yet none of these filters down to the small business owner. Managing your own business, you must wear many hats and cyber security is rarely one of them. CyberPie is a simple solution that wraps up the best tools, tips and tales into a subscription tailored to the unique needs of the small business owner and entrepreneur.

s I enter the second half of my life (yes, I plan to live to 100) I've never felt a stronger sense purpose and clarity in my career choice. I have the best of both worlds - the freedom to ild the business I want, and the knowledge that I've found the thing that sizzles my con—cyber security.

hat I have learnt:

- ☐ Fortune favours the Brave.

- ☐ Be the change you want to see.

- ☐ Find what sizzles your bacon, then find your niche within that.

- ☐ Seek out help, the cyber security/infosec community is very generous and supportive.

- ☐ Always be learning and re-skilling.

- ☐ Read, write, and seek out speaking opportunities; they are out there.

- ☐ There is no shame in starting out again or starting over.

- ☐ If necessity is the mother of invention, age is the mother of reinvention.

Chapter 3

Name: Pooja Agrawalla

Job Title: IAM Leader

Company: Leading Semiconductor Manufacturer

Location: Bangalore, Karnataka, India

Can't wait for tomorrow, as I get better every day!

The Woman, I am – a poem by Absent Wryta.

"Some say I am a strong woman,
Some tell me I am a brave woman,
Some think I should be more of a woman,
Some will tell you I'm a good woman,
While some think I'm not much of a woman,
Or at all like any woman they ever knew,
And that I could be so much more.

But all I am is a woman,
All I am is my woman,
I am the woman I can be,
The one I want to be,
Not the one I should be, could be, would be,
Not so much more, too much like or nearly so".

Since COVID-19, the US FBI registered a 300% increase in reported cybercrimes. Unfilled cybersecurity jobs worldwide are already over 4 million. Meanwhile, women make up only 11-20% of the cybersecurity workforce. What does this mean? IT IS TIME we make the demographics correct. There is a lot of opportunity to be seized in cybersecurity careers for women. In this context, I am going to share my story, so that you may get some tips from my transition and career journey.

I am Pooja Agrawalla. I work on Identity and Access Management (IAM), a domain of cyber security. I am an Indian and live in Bangalore, India. Apart from my work, I am part of various cybersecurity and women communities and networks. My other roles are as a daughter, a sister, a mother, and a wife.

Let us start with a little background of my childhood. I belong to an educated and open-minded family; my father was a doctor and my mother a homemaker. Father was a traveller, who later decided to settle in a small town in India, where I grew up and got an education. A small Indian town may add more challenges for women. I have seen instances where girls could not pursue higher education, because their parents wanted them to get married. The risk of finding a relatively higher qualified groom was always a consideration for a girl's education. Despite this, my life has been a sheer privilege. I am indebted to my parents, for making me independent and decisive. From childhood, I have tuned myself to decide and deal with outcomes on my own.

I completed my engineering in "computer science" in 2001. A day in engineering was when I saw computers for the first time. It was also the first time I got to touch one. It happened during computer lab time. Our college had only a few computers, each to be shared by 2-3 students. I remember it was Windows 95 machine. I learnt MS-DOS and created my first folder using commands, and wow! it felt like a big achievement. I was in love with computers at first sight. Now, a decade later, I am doing an M-Tech in computing infrastructure. But it all started from that moment, my first day with computers!

After my graduation, a few events like the World Trade Tower and Pentagon Attack, and 2001 recession changed everything I planned for. My first job offer was cancelled, and the recession affected all possibilities of getting a new job. I am sure, like me some of you also at multiple times would have consciously embraced failures and setbacks and did not let it hold us back. Accepting failure and setback is the very first step. Working hard is next. If I continued to fail it could have led me to a horrible future. It could have led me to an undesired marriage. Imagine my life then, it would be without any self-identity, with no right to choose, being voiceless in this male-dominant society. Scary as it sounds; failing again was not an option for me. I believe for all of us, bouncing back is always an option. It may be hard but not impossible. To consider this option, I moved to a city. I was jobless and for few weeks I was running at the expense of my father. Sustaining and funding my own expenses, become my priority. I managed to get my first job, which paid me ~$100 a month. I worked double shift to manage work, training, and learning. Thankfully the first breakthrough came when I landed a "dream job" with an American multinational technology and consulting company, as a Mainframe Software Engineer.

Out of many other things in this job, my most favourite one, was the first time when I handled a critical escalation or a "crisis situation". I was managing an insurance pay-out system, which prints checks to customers based on their claims. The escalation was due to a production issue, where the pay-out system was printing older checks. Everyone including my management was focused to find the root cause and communicate it to client stakeholders. Pressure was extremely high. What happens next could impact my company's relationship with client. A young me, used "foolish courage" to commit in solving the issue. One of my strengths is my ability to learn and solve problems. Learning quickly, doing step by step analysis and connecting threads helped in identifying the root cause. I was not hesitant to share correct information. Most importantly I was not withholding any information.

Multiple times, escalations have become opportunities for me. I have learnt that with commitment, learning, flexibility, and transparency you can manage any situations. Interestingly, according to study 'Psychology of Women Quarterly', women because of their interpersonal skills are better leaders during a crisis. A good example of this could be seen during the COVID-19 crisis. We already know that countries led by women have witnessed fewer deaths compared to the ones with similar characteristics led by men. I would request all women leaders who are reading this article to make use of such crisis opportunities to shine and get visible.

I like to code and did a lot of it, though it was mostly in the early part of my career. In addition to legacy languages, having good understanding of object-oriented languages helped. I gradually upgraded to newer languages (even today, out of my own interest). I was reading an article that claimed that women are better coders, and their code, gets accepted more often. This research was done on GitHub where name and email id were co-related to various social websites. Note - GitHub does not maintain Gender in its data. This article made me think- "Why do women self-doubt and not get fair recognition?". It is time to make yourself heard. Make noise using your codes. Please innovate and code. Codes like ideas, do not wait. If we will not do it then someone else will. To all the women who code, more power to you.

I want to share another interesting phase of my career. This is when I switched from Mainframe to Cyber Security i.e., IAM. That switch was not what I planned. I did not know anything about Cyber Security or IAM. From a coder, who was writing COBOL and JCLs, I must now implement IAM solutions and products. As interesting it may sound; this was not an easy switch. I had to start again, unlearn, and learn. The first few weeks were a whirlwind. During early days, IAM was mostly done using Active Directory. Soon, enterprise tools for automated provisioning and lifecycle management for IAM were introduced. Some of the early products came from CA, IBM, Sun, and Novel. When I started with IAM, there were very few people implementing IAM products. Outlook for these products and IAM was not known, and I realized the risk I had taken with my career. Trusting my abilities, I decided to work towards mitigating the risk. My familiarity with Java, servlets and JSPs, helped a lot with these products. To manage the transition, getting an understanding of the product's architecture was my first step. I was aware of application development fundamental concepts like design patterns, MVC architecture, and it helped me in designing solutions. I remember opening jar files of these products to read and understand the code. You will be surprised to know - I was also training others, while learning. It helped me in validating my own learnings. Gradually step by step, I was able to contribute more. Reflecting on this transition, I consider it as my second breakthrough. This decision in moving to Identity and cybersecurity, made me what I am today. If I can do it, I believe you can too.

Talking about Identity and cybersecurity, every bit of this job can be done by a woman. From writing codes to reviews, attending a security incident to threat hunting, keeping systems updated to identifying threats to innovate and improve, all of that can be done by a woman. Please do not get intimated; move forward to take your chances. You should embrace learning and agility in this field. All women should know that their skills and perspectives are wanted and needed in cybersecurity. While it is challenging; it is also extremely rewarding.

Moving on, amongst these professional juggles, I also went through key phases of my personal life. I got married and started a beautiful family. Looking back to a quote of from my favourite leader Indra Nooyi, where she says, "*Women cannot have it all*". I do not agree. If a woman makes her own choices, and more so does it with no guilt; I believe "*she can have it all*". A woman can integrate and have it all. A common problem for women is "Super Woman Syndrome", where a super woman is said to have "unusual" abilities to do it all. Superwoman is a fictional character, not a role model, and trying to be her can lead to stress both physically and mentally. I have avoided this syndrome, by saying "No" and by not only asking, but also demanding help. Start saying no to things that you do not want, or do not have the time, to do.

In my career, I got to experience global culture during my stay in US. Having a global career and international outlook is a bonus for me. It led me to my next job, as a consultant in one of the BIG 4 firms. I had to work with global teams and deliver solutions as one team. Additionally, being a consultant, I had to adapt quickly to any style, methodology, and solution. To help with adaptation, it is important we identify our strengths early on. It helps in planning the next steps. I am an organized person, and this helped me in adapting quickly to agility. In this role, I implemented new identity administration products, new areas like Privileged Identity Management and virtual directories for few big clients.

During this tenure I experienced loneliness for the first time. I was the only woman present in many forums/meetings/events. The global problem of diversity is much worse in consulting. Being part of a minority group can make you feel like an outsider, even more so if your male colleagues are older or more senior than you. I was able to survive this phase by being persistent in my goals. I have learnt that in such meetings and forums; good preparation, paying attention, and speaking up usually helps. I usually either ask questions or make a recommendation, but always try to speak up.

Sharing another instance when I was setting up team for a project. I initially got a male team leader. Later a few more male colleagues joined the team. As the leader of this team and with intent to bring diversity, I recruited a lady consultant to it. I still remember, how everyone opposed my decision. There was apprehension that a woman may delay deliverables. She will not know and must be taught first. Doubts were whether a woman could manage pressure and work long hours. We must fight such bias and perceptions! In my case, I was empowered to decide to include her in the team. I left the rest to her. As I expected, she proved all of them wrong. Do you notice how women must prove their abilities again and again? Many companies showcase their heroic efforts to increase diversity and inclusion. In my opinion, talks and numbers could only be a "lip-service", and inclusion is far from their reach. Inclusion must start from top management, from mind and then behaviour.

This incident also made me think... "Are women enabling these thoughts, by opting for less stressful jobs?". I do not think it is an ambition problem. Women are considered to be ambitious. But then why do we settle for less? I would like you to pause and think about that. Please self-reflect and understand your strengths and weakness. Use your strengths to capture your fears. Do not be self-critical and underestimate your own potential. Advocate yourself and embrace tough assignments. More women stepping up confidently and competitively in challenging roles, will set examples for others. Top management if reading this, please tune your diversity and inclusion programs to address these gaps. Imagine a future, where we do not have to prove our abilities to others, to get included.

Growth as a subject matter expert is also important. To do this there could be two approaches. Vertical or horizontal. Vertical is becoming an expert in one solution, whereas horizontal is exploring and knowing just enough from all solutions. I started off using the vertical approach, focussing on Sun Microsystems Identity Management products. Later on, I started moving more horizontally to get enough information on other solutions. Using that approach, I was able to explore IBM Tivoli IAM suite, Oracle IAM products including Oracle LDAP, Oracle virtual directories and privileged access management products like CyberArk.

My leadership journey started a few years back, when I stepped into a leadership role leading the IAM group for a financial company (non-US offices). This role required me to manage a function, its managers, and teams. Earlier I was solving client/customers problem, but now I had to look/find/solve problems within the company. Technically I was strong, and this role made me realize the importance of being functional. By learning and adapting functional skills, I expanded my understanding on risks, business problems, big picture view and could visualize connections between multiple problems. By looking beyond IAM I also got to understand other cybersecurity areas. Leadership journey in my opinion, takes all we know so far, expands, and integrates it with other related areas, and moves it to the next stage. It empowers you to plan strategic outcomes for yourself and for your team.

The number of women in leadership roles are very few and its overly concerning. Listen to Emma Watson's speech in UN. She says, *"The reality is that if we do nothing it will take 75 years, or for me to be nearly a hundred before women can expect to be paid the same as men for the same work"*. Whenever I listen to her, every cell of my body wants to do more. While the representation of women in leadership roles is on the rise, the process is indeed slow. India is at least a decade behind the global countries and ranks fifth lowest in having women at top leadership positions. Like you I cannot wait a lifetime for it, meaning that together we must move fast to close the gap in our own lifetime.

In my leadership journey, I was fortunate to have great friends and mentors. I want to emphasize how mentors and friends are a big factor in your personal and professional growth. A best friend at work can work wonders on your motivation and happiness levels. The point I want to make is sometimes it is important not to limit conversations only to official matters. Give time to understand a colleague; it will help in building strong relationships. To do this, I usually do "walk meetings". It helps me to relax to allow more open discussions. Workplace friends continue to be my real-life friends.

On mentoring, I am sure I will not be the first one talking about it. You would have heard this from others. I sing the same song. Everyone should look for a mentor or sponsor. Find a mentor who is just a few years ahead of you in their professional/personal journey. It will help in relating experiences. While you get mentored, I would also recommend you to be a mentor. Becoming a mentor to someone will help you exercise your own emotional intelligence. By mentoring women, I could re-apply my learnings and re-affirms my beliefs.

Another important factor - "Learning". It is my strongest pillar. I am a passionate learner. I want to be the most qualified, learned and educated women. While working, I enrolled and

mpleted programs such as PGDBA, a Diploma for Design thinking and a few
rtifications. I am currently pursuing an M-Tech. I got certified as Scrum master, CISSP,
CSP, SAfe product owner. On the job/fly learning is key in transition to new roles or areas.
believe in setting learning goals to push oneself. For anyone who is aspiring to join Cyber
curity, my suggestion is to learn and get a good understanding of computing infrastructure
 Applications, OS, Databases, platforms, and networks. Learning one or two programming
nguages will always help. For leadership roles, Risk Management skills are very essential.
earning without applying is like "window shopping". Einstein said "*Any fool can know. The
int is to understand*". I would add "*The point is to understand and apply*". It is not easy to
t on everything you read or learn. You have read this story, but it is unlikely you will apply
e information that you have read so far. To help you apply, I would ask each of you to take
tip, with which you connected the most. Write it on a piece of paper. Every morning and
hile working read and use the tip. Do this at least for a week. By applying, most likely you
ill not forget it.

oming back to my journey, today I am with a company that values my contributions and
lfils me every single day. I have a good team and I am empowered to deliver.
uthentication, access controls, privileged access have been in the top 10 threats for
bersecurity. Traditional IAM will no longer work. The time is now to switch to next-gen
eas of IAM i.e., moving to Passwordless options, using biometrics, getting rid of the
count itself - Just in time access, implement Federation and SCIM provisioning, securing
oud with IAM controls, using IAM Fabrics, and introducing Zero trust culture. I am
xcited as I get to work and promote these advanced areas. What more could I ask?

y story would not be complete, If I do not mention my bosses. When I look back at the
aders I worked with, I have had mixed experiences with both good and bad leaders.
nfortunately, all my bosses were male; I have not experienced female leadership yet. A few
od ones have made a big impact on my life. One of them is my mentor, to whom I look up
 for advice. Bad ones have also made an impact, as I know exactly what I should not be
ing as a leader. In general, it is a fact that most leaders are men. This means we need to be
reful as we grow as a leader. All historic lessons and leadership programs are mostly
cused on men, and primarily aim to make women emulate men. I strongly believe that
hen women are different (especially when different from men), they perform better as
aders. It is important to be yourself, and not emulate others as you grow.

regret starting late with networking. Once I started, I realized its benefits. I strongly suggest
 utilizing like-minded networks. It provides social support, friendship and a sense of
ciprocity that can itself be empowering. My mentor gave me a useful tip in networking.
hen you approach networking, always offer more to others. Keeping inward motives, will
t help you network. As you begin to start offering to others, you will be surprised on how
uch you are getting back. In cyber security there are many events which are either free or
ry affordable. Apply for scholarships, seek sponsorship, self-invest but make a point to
tend at least 1-2 events in a year. Give out more by writing a blog or by being active on
cial platforms such as LinkedIn. I am glad about the network I have gained over the past
w years. I meet people who share the same passion as me and learn from their experiences.
am passionate for pro-bono/volunteering work in various communities for women and cyber
curity. I have participated and contributed to various communities. Be it GHCI India, where
vo of my papers were selected, or working as EWF India core team in arranging events and

sessions for women in cybersecurity. I also work as a core member of CSA Bangalore chapter. My contributions were recognized recently when I was awarded Top 20 Indian Women Influencer in Security 2020, by SecurityToday, InfosecGirls and WISECRA.

Apart from work and other things, I also make time for my hobbies and health. To be best at work, one needs to de-stress mind and body. I like biographies, history, and real-life stories. I read or watch them in my free times. I love travelling to explore different culture and nature. From my travel log, one of the best places I have visited is "Pangong lake" in Leh, Ladakh, India. Gardening and writing are a few other things I like to do.

In the end, anyone can have a "once upon a time" or a "happily ever after" story, but I believe it is the journey between that makes the story worth telling. In my journey, I am enjoying the present. When I look back at the past, I get inspirations from many strong leaders (especially women). I can't wait for tomorrow, as I get better every day!

A few of my important tips with few one liner statements for easy application are summarised below. Do reach out to me personally (using LinkedIn) if you think I can help/support you in your journey.

- Be confident and competent. Remember others could be worse than you.
- Accept failure and prepare for future.
- To have it all, make choices guilt free.
- Please remember, you are not a Super Woman!
- Embrace tough assignments!
- Adapt continuous learning and stay relevant.
- Find a mentor and be a mentor.
- Make best friends at work.
- Network, Network and Network!
- Do not emulate others, use your differences.
- Take out time for hobbies and health.

Chapter 4

Name: Caroline G. Ndege

Title: Cyber Security Specialist

Company: None

Location: Nairobi, Kenya

<u>Cybersecurity, I love it here!</u>

Formative Years:

Throughout my schooling years, I've been consistently inclined towards Mathematics and Science studies. I had a supportive family and teachers, both of whom shaped my inquisitive mindset immensely from an early age. Their reassurance greatly helped me, as it pushed me to bounce back whenever I felt my studies were a bit too heavy on me. I feel eternally indebted to them and, in return, I also extended help to my classmates through avenues such as study groups, pre-examination classwork revision and the like.

Higher Education Phase:

I performed well at my O-Levels and received admission into a great university, as a government- sponsored student, where I enrolled on a degree course in Computer Science. Suffice to say the main degree options at this learning institution were STEM-based. I was thrilled and unsettled at the same time, as I had only interacted with a handful of women, who held qualifications along the lines of my selected course.

My reality while undertaking studies, was that the female students' population in my class and in other STEM classes offered in my institution was extremely low (less than a third of the total). My lady friends in Engineering class were not spared this actuality either; for example, there were only some 5 of them in a class of 30. At some point, a few felt so misplaced they contemplated dropping out their Engineering courses, to join alternative courses that were considered 'feminine' and bearable. The mother to one of the lady students intervened after she expressed her discontentment with the Engineering field. Periodically, she (the mother) would drive to campus, about 2 hours away from her workplace, meet the ladies in their cubicle in the halls of residence and encourage them to soldier on with STEM studies. Hers was an invaluable sacrifice, and yes, the ladies triumphed!

It took grit for me as a woman to work through my campus studies as well, as from time to time I'd wonder what the STEM job market would look like, given that women were so gravely outnumbered in the class environment.

At the Workplace:
On graduating, I got employment in the Banking industry, and a few months down the line switched over to an Information Systems Internal Audit role. My observations on the glaring gender disparities (number-wise) in this new environment were upheld. Whenever I'd head over to the ICT Department for audit assignments, I'd notice females were also quite few in number there. At this point, it sadly hit me that there was a huge gap in women in STEM employment too, a direct result of the low numbers enrolled in Science-based courses at universities, tertiary colleges and even those in tech-based apprenticeships. Others easily dropped out ICT, primarily due to work/family-life balance. It was quite an intimidating experience, working in a new job in an office that was male dominated, while simultaneously focusing ahead and realizing also that there were hardly any women in the leadership roles. As I planned out my future in IT, I settled on networking with co-workers and peers; as a team we'd raise each other's morale to carry on delivering tasks.

A few years later, I changed jobs, becoming a Cyber Security Specialist, aiming to gain more exposure in matters relating to handling ICT risks. It's quite a challenging line, but my willingness to carry on learning keeps me going. Additionally, with most businesses focusing on automation means the demand for cyber professionals keeps rising; I'm happy to lend my skills! Technical skills and exposure to the trending cyber patterns most definitely came in handy. I credit my first boss, in the cyber department for consistently availing opportunities to sharpen my proficiency in both areas.

However, even in instances where one isn't quite competent, I like encouraging women to enrol in online study programs (some of which are free), which easily cater for individuals from diverse professional backgrounds. Those programs are also flexible enough to allow the individual to study at her own pace, making it an especially workable option. Communication and interpersonal skills also come in handy and they can be cultivated as one goes about one's social life.

Though there's slight improvement in women taking up STEM-based careers, there are still not too many visible women in the Cybersecurity profession which is truly disheartening. From my perspective, people thrive better by observing those with whom they can identify; this spurred me on to connect with Cyber enthusiasts through online forums, some exclusively for women and others whose members are drawn from both genders. They have helped my growth immensely.

Beyond the Office:

I always grab the chance to cheer women who are new entrants to the Cybersecurity arena, something that led me about a year ago to volunteer time and skills to run such a newly launched program for an International Professional body in my city. In executing the program's mandate, I would collaborate with like-minded organizations/professional women/male allies in motivating young campus students to embrace STEM. It warms my heart, to know that there is a wider variety of options for the current generation of young women than there was back then to obtain STEM information and whom to look up to.

This initiative is also an excellent platform for women from various backgrounds to gain the opportunity to share their Cyber stories, for the benefit of others.

Learning Points:

One of the psych-up quotes I like is Lao Tzu's *"The journey of a thousand miles begins with one step"*. Alongside this, I'd like to share some guides that keep me on track as I explore the options available in my professional journey:

- You may not have a complete map as you set out on your Cyber career: start off anyway.
- Continuously seek career growth and personal empowerment opportunities, and where possible pull along your fellow young women.
- Explore mentorship options, the right mentor will provide you unmatched career advice.
- Strive to be professionally ready, so you confidently embrace career opportunities as they come along.
- Where necessary, press pause, it's allowed! Just don't lose focus on your professional goals and aspirations.

All Said and Done:

The Cybersecurity path may not always be linear. However, I'm positive that in the near future, more women will boldly join ,and persist in, the Cyber World and through their knowledge and skills, help to create a safer Cyber Space.

Cheers, to the brilliant women in Cyber around the globe!

Chapter 5

Name: Sai Honig

Job Title: Cofounder

Company Name: New Zealand Network for Women in Security (non-profit)

Location: Wellington, New Zealand

> "Two roads diverged in a yellow wood,
> And sorry I could not travel both
> And be one traveler, long I stood
> And looked down one as far as I could
> To where it bent in the undergrowth;"   Robert Frost

My career into cybersecurity was definitely non-linear. I did not come into it with a degree in computer science or masters in cybersecurity. I did not work at a security tools provider or software company. As I look back, I learned that I am a multi-potentialite. I worked in other careers. I learned something from each of these previous careers that I carry into cybersecurity. Cybersecurity is my third career. I took the road "not taken".

As a child, I didn't know that such a profession existed. Computers were just coming into daily life. I was fortunate to attend a rural elementary school that was able to purchase a classroom of TRS-80's. At home, I was fortunate to have an IBM PC. I remember spending hours at school and at home on these machines writing simple programs. I even created a cypher program to disguise notes that I sent to one friend.

In high school, I elected to take programming classes. These weren't the languages that we use now. The point was to learn how to think like machines.

or my bachelor's degree, I did take more programming courses. I did see students in omputer science, but it seemed that all they did was stay indoors and code. It wasn't of any iterest to me.

t that time, my interest was in aerospace engineering. I watched as the Challenger shuttle lew up after launch. At that time, I wanted to design the next generation space shuttle that 'ould prevent such disasters. I obtained a Bachelor's degree in aerospace engineering.

started working for a contractor that had some work with NASA. I was able to work on rojects where I could design components and subsystems. I learned 3D design and drafting. ne project required that I send designs securely to an external party. So, I learned about icryption and networks. I still didn't know about cybersecurity as a profession.

became disillusioned about my prospects to grow and work on projects that interested me. I :e now that my gender and race probably played a part in restricting my upward movement r being assigned interesting projects. Despite receiving recognition from within the ompany and from external customers, my manager told me that I was not eligible for a igher-level role because I did not have formal business education. I took his words :riously. I did not realize then that those who were in that higher level role I wanted also did ot have formal business education.

quit about six months later, I enrolled in an MBA in international management. This rogram accepted that I did not have a traditional background for an MBA program. The rogram also allowed me to study language and cross-cultural communication. This was mething not common in MBA programs at that time. I also studied abroad in Prague and eneva and hoped to work in another country after graduating.

fter graduating with this MBA, I started working for multinational corporations with offices the US and elsewhere. I was based in the US in the role of internal audit. This meant :viewing financial statements and supporting transactions to verify their validity. I had the pportunity to travel for work to other parts of the world for short intervals. However, I did anage a few weekends to explore.

arbanes-Oxley Act came into effect in July 2002. This act increased the responsibilities as 1 internal auditor. As part of the requirements of the act, review of technical controls that npacted financial reporting was required. So as a financial internal auditor, I had to get to now IT systems. I learned about C-I-A triad, access management, key transactions pprovals, governance, application security basics, plus a whole lot more.

ater I worked for a regional hospital system that implemented end-to-end electronic medical :cords. It was amazing to see how better care could be provided when the right data was /ailable at the patient's bedside. Because this system held patient data, I quickly learned :quirements of privacy under HIPAA. This was an aspect of cybersecurity that I also dived :eply into. While I was there, I obtained my CISA (Certified Information Systems Auditor), /en then I did not feel that I was working in cybersecurity.

was first introduced to cloud technology while working at a retail pharmacy company. I as not sure what to expect. I was just told that the marketing director had this new system to track sales and contracts. When I met with him, it was clear that his excitement overlooked some very basic cybersecurity standards. Standards such as least privilege, access management, change controls and others. I began by talking about~~to him~~ what additional controls his new system needed.

Since I was new to cloud technology, I wasn't really sure where to start in securing it. (I even asked if I could get a new assignment but was told that I had to figure it out.) I sat down at my workstation and typed "cloud security" into a search window. What came up was Cloud Security Alliance®.

This was an organization of cybersecurity professionals figuring out how to use cloud technology securely. These professionals volunteered their time to prepare guidance based on their experience and research. I came across their "Security Guidance", which set out very clearly the steps to be reviewed and implemented when using cloud technologies. Version 4 is available today and is built on previous iterations of the security guidance, dedicated research, public participation from the Cloud Security Alliance members, working groups, and the industry experts. I can honestly say that if I had not found Cloud Security Alliance and that document, I ~~would~~ probably would not have continued to study cloud technology.

I was really impressed with Cloud Security Alliance ®, that I helped set up a chapter in Phoenix, Arizona, USA. That was 2013. It's still going strong!

One of my passions is microfinance. I am impressed with how processes developed by Grameen Bank have empowered the poorest to improve their lives and reduce extreme poverty. Grameen Bank started Grameen Foundation with the purpose of sharing that knowledge gained and helping other organizations. I volunteered my skills to the Foundation and helped them develop IT processes for their global offices and their risk matrix and audit programs. (All of this was on a cloud platform). I was just very happy to be a small part of doing some good in a global setting. I was very surprised to be a recipient of the US President's Volunteer Service Award in 2013. This award recognizes the contributions of volunteers and encourages others to engage in volunteer service. This award included a letter from then President Barack Obama!

What I also quickly realized is that talking about cybersecurity to a marketing director was not like talking to cybersecurity with a developer or an architect. I could not just tell him that he needed to implement controls. I needed to explain why and use language that he could understand.

Someone once asked me "What is your cybersecurity superpower?" I said that it was my ability to speak to people, both technical and non-technical, about the need for cybersecurity.

I took the CISSP exam in October 2013 even though I did not yet have the full 5 years' experience. I was able to take the exam as an Associate of (ISC)^2. I sat the exam because I wanted to show the world, and the profession, that I was serious about working in cybersecurity. I passed and received the Associate designation.

Even though I was auditing IT systems and cloud implementations, I really wasn't seen as a cybersecurity professional. I got tired not seeing my career grow. I did reach out and ask for mentorship, but no one was willing to see my potential.

Working in the United States can be difficult. There are very few holidays and little vacation time. Expectations are that you work far more than the usual 40 hours per week. I felt I was always struggling to keep up with the work and never really be able to enjoy any downtime because of exhaustion. I knew that life should be easier.

Looking at other countries, New Zealand seemed to have an appreciation of the quality of life and work/life balance. There was also a need for my skillset. So, in October 2012, husband (a Ph.D. psychologist) and I made the trip to New Zealand. Before going, we reached out to recruiters and did some research. While visiting, I attended a conference and made connections. Once we got back to the US, we started the long and arduous process to immigrate. During that process, I kept in touch with some of the connections I made while I was waiting for the immigration process to complete.

Once I received approval to immigrate in 2014, I started the job search process and applying for jobs. I met with recruiters. One recruiter was really discouraging. She said that I did not have credentials even after I pointed out that I had certifications!

Shortly after arriving in New Zealand, I was invited to meet with a Professor Ryan Ko, Ph. D at Waikato University. He invited me to write a chapter in a book, which I did since I did not have a job. I had not written anything longer than a few pages. Now I was asked to write a complete chapter! The book would be published about a year later.

I was still concerned that I would not be considered a cybersecurity professional. However, one connection I had made a few years earlier encouraged me to apply for a specific position. I applied for the job and was accepted! I became a security manager for a hospital system on the North Island of New Zealand. It was my first job in New Zealand; I also considered it my first job in cybersecurity.

During my time there, I was able to complete the necessary experience to convert the Associate of (ISC)^2 to a CISSP (Certified Information Systems Security Professional) ® in October 2015. I was also able to study for the CCSP® (Certified Cloud Security Professional). I passed the exam and received the CCSP® in December that year.

Almost a year later, in October 2016, I was invited to speak at Cloud Asia in Singapore. The invitation was given by Cloud Security Alliance®. I spoke about a project being conducted at the district health board I was working at. The project was an experiment to use cloud technology to improve access to health care in a rural and widely dispersed population. To say that I was petrified is an understatement. I was a dark-skinned, female, American speaking about a project in New Zealand in front of a global stage in Singapore. After arriving at the conference, I was told that not only was I going to give a talk but would also be speaking on a panel.

I was really surprised at the reaction at Cloud Asia. I met with many in the Asia region who were interested in what I had to say. My biggest surprise was meeting David Shearer. He was the CEO of $(ISC)^2$. He said he was impressed with my ability to speak about cloud technology and speak on a panel. He asked if I would consider becoming a board member of $(ISC)^2$! I was given just a few days to consider this option.

Talking to my husband at the end of the first day, I told him about meeting David Shearer and he is asking me to consider becoming a board member $(ISC)^2$. My husband listened intently and then asked, "Well, you read the book "Lean In". Are you going to lean in?". This is what happens when you are married to a psychologist!

I did see this opportunity to lean in and be seen as a leader. The process to become a board member is a long one. There was no guarantee that at the end of the process, I would be successful. As it turned out, I was successful. In January 2017, I became one of 13 board members of $(ISC)^2$!

For the next three years, I had to represent over 140,000 members worldwide to the management. This meant that I had to travel once per quarter from New Zealand to meet members and attend conferences. My favorite part was meeting students and those new to cybersecurity. Their enthusiasm was contagious and reminded me of why I decided on this profession. Although I did not have a mentor, I decided to mentor others.

Despite being on an international board, many in New Zealand did not see me as a leader. Worse still, I had people, working in cybersecurity, tell me directly that I was *not* a cybersecurity professional. This dug at me deeply. In 2019, my position was eliminated at the company where I worked. I was in my final year as a board member of the largest information security professional member organization. But I was ready to quit.

I took about four months away from the profession. During that time, I explored other fields such as machine learning and blockchain. I wrote a little bit. I picked up the flute again and toyed with the idea of studying jazz. I read history books that focused on Black America.

I also took time to meet people for a chat. In Wellington, it's common to go for a coffee and have a chat. When I look back at that time, the people I met were those with whom I had worked but were not in cybersecurity. They reminded me how I interacted with them and their teams. They reminded me that my superpower was and still is the ability to speak about cybersecurity to non-cybersecurity professionals. No one felt they were beneath me. Some even said that I took away the fear of cybersecurity. Now they think about how to apply cybersecurity principles in their work.

During this time, I had started reading a book written by Ted Demopoulos called "Infosec Rock Star: How to Accelerate Your Career Because Geek Will Only Get You So Far". Ted's book really grabbed hold of me. In it, I saw that I had become a cybersecurity professional (maybe not the rock star). My cybersecurity superpower did mean something.

During my time as a board member of $(ISC)^2$, I also saw that other countries had successful groups of women in security. In New Zealand, we did have women in technology but nothing focusing on security. This is a challenging profession but there was no forum to reach out to others. We also had students who did not have role models or may not understand the full range of jobs in cybersecurity.

So, with my good friend, Tash Bettridge, we started the New Zealand Network for Women in Security (NZNWS). We received support from Women in Security (WoSec) in the US.

Cloud Security Alliance® (CSA) is a global organization of professional members in the cloud technology community. CSA conducts research in different aspects of technology. In early 2020, I was asked to join the CSA's Asia Pacific Research Advisory Council for the research conducted in Asia. This provided me with insight into potentially new and emerging technologies!

With NZNWS, we started 2020 with optimism and had a few in-person sessions. Mostly, it was to get to know who was interested and what they might be interested in. We did not charge to be a member because we knew that cost could be a barrier. We also had students reach out to us and were able to get some connections made. Mostly, we wanted it to grow organically.

Then came the Covid-19 lockdown in late March. A nation of fewer than 5 million people went to full lockdown. The borders were already closed but we all had "stay at home orders" in place which were enforced. This meant no meeting for coffee or catching up after work. No sports. Schooling and work were conducted at home. We lined up (socially distanced) at grocery stores, pharmacies, and pet food stores. We shared bread recipes. We put teddy bears and other stuffed animals in our windows to cheer each other up from a distance.

Daily updates from the Prime Minister and Director General of Health and Zoom® meetings became the norm. After several weeks, the orders were eased, and we enjoyed our takeaways. Still, we social distanced and worked and schooled from home. It was not until early June before the restrictions in the country were removed. However, the borders still remained closed.

During this time, the NZNWS met online. We had deep conversations about life as we knew it. We talked about the challenges we were facing and how we could help each other. Some shared their personal stories.

In 2020, it seemed that everyone was working harder than before, including me. I was also studying for another certification and spent months cramming for it. (I even put aside studying jazz flute to focus on it.) Because I have dyslexia, exams can be difficult. As was my practice, I stopped studying two days before the exam just to reduce my anxiety. I didn't pass. I know this does not mean that I'm incompetent. It just means I was not ready. Still, my confidence did take its toll on me.

I continued with NZNWS and with CSA's Asia Pacific Research Advisory Council. I continued to speak about security and technology and work as a security consultant. I continued to study and practise jazz flute.

2020 was a year where my racial resiliency was at an all-time low. I had watched the pandemic in the US take a disproportionate number of people of color. I watched the protests after Black Americans were killed by police. I saw the racist comments and videos directed at people who looked at me. It reminded me of all the injustices I had experienced when living in the US. I had to put all those emotions aside and go to work. I had also been a victim of racial injustice several times while living in New Zealand. When I hear "white privilege" comments (or worse), I had to turn the other cheek and pretend it was ok. When I did call it out, I was told to calm down. I was tired of crying alone in a corner. I retreated from many people except the very few who understood and could feel the same.

In October 2020, I joined Black Cybersecurity Alliance (BCA). BCA is an inclusive non-profit organization focused on community, and career mentorship for underrepresented minorities in the cybersecurity industry. My reason for joining was to be part of something that could accept the whole me. I did not have to pretend and hold back when I was put down because of race. For the first time, I knew and felt that I was seen as someone who was a cybersecurity professional. I was someone who others aspire to and emulate. It was the first time I was asked to mentor others who looked like me. I felt very privileged to share my story.

Then in late 2020, I was notified that I was an IFSEC Global 2020 Cybersecurity Influencer! I'm not sure who nominated me, but the selection was made by highly respected judges – peers in the field! Later, I was selected for another recognition - Women in Security Awards Aotearoa 2020. This was newly established to recognize women who have advanced the New Zealand security industry. Both recognitions helped me to see that I was accepted by others as a cybersecurity professional.

I finally accepted that I was a cybersecurity professional. My journey here has been long but not direct. I'm proud of what I have accomplished, honored to have been recognized and look forward to continuing the work. My thoughts are to those, particularly women, who are interested in coming into cybersecurity. It is a field for those who are bold and willing to challenge the status quo. Be willing to *have an open mind* and *do your research*. Be willing to put yourself out there and be ready to be challenged! We live in a world that is currently challenged on many fronts. Those challenges require big thinking. Take the skills you have and build on them.

I thank those that have been a part of my journey and encouraged me to find my way. I thank my husband, Larry Honig, for reminding me that I am a beautiful human whenever I forget.

So, the poem that started this chapter, really describes my journey:

> Two roads diverged in a yellow wood,
> And sorry I could not travel both
> And be one traveler, long I stood
> And looked down one as far as I could
> To where it bent in the undergrowth;
>
> Then took the other, as just as fair,
> And having perhaps the better claim,
> Because it was grassy and wanted wear;
> Though as for that the passing there

Had worn them really about the same,

And both that morning equally lay
In leaves no step had trodden black.
Oh, I kept the first for another day!
Yet knowing how way leads on to way,
I doubted if I should ever come back.

I shall be telling this with a sigh
Somewhere ages and ages hence:
Two roads diverged in a wood, and I—
I took the one less traveled by,
And that has made all the difference.   Robert Frost

The world needs people like you to stand up and stand out!

Chapter 6

Name: Yatia (Tia) Hopkins

Job Title: Vice President of Global Solutions Engineering

Company: eSentire, Inc.

Location: Long Island, New York

For as long as I can remember, I was never as interested in using something as I was in knowing how it worked. I always wanted to take things apart, inspect all of the pieces, and put them back together. I began disassembling my younger brother's toy trucks at the age of 8; I was extremely curious about what was inside. A few years later, that same curiosity possessed me to disassemble my first computer immediately after my mother bought it for m because she realized I was fascinated with them.

Needless to say, the day I disassembled my first computer was also the same day I built my first computer. My mother was less than pleased when she walked into my room and saw what, to her, looked like a pile of junk and a waste of her hard-earned money; she demanded put it back together, of course. Looking back, I realize that moment lit a fire in me that is still burning today, nearly thirty years later. Sadly, as a child I didn't have the guidance or access to resources that would've helped me channel my technical energy, hone my skills, and find path. So, when I was older, I had to forge my own.

I was born in Richmond, VA; the oldest of three children and raised by a single mother for most of my early childhood. My mom was (and still is) an incredibly strong woman. She was determined to protect and provide for her children by any means necessary. I had no idea at the time but watching her struggle, persevere, and not give up time after time planted the seeds in my mind that anything was possible, and that no challenge could ever be greater than my will to overcome.

When I was 11, my family (including my new stepfather) left Virginia and moved to North Carolina. After a short period, we relocated again, to South Carolina. This period in my life (middle school through high school graduation) began to shape the woman I became and how I approached situations in life.

I was enrolled in advanced classes in school, and always favored mathematics. I was often the only black student in my class, so not only did I not "fit in" with my classmates, I also didn't fit in with the other black students because I was in the "special" or "uppity" classes. To them, I was considered too "white" or an "Oreo." To make matters worse, I didn't really share similar interests with many of my peers. For example, I remember being called a nerd because I decided to join the Math Team. Who in their right mind solves math problems for fun, right? And it's certainly not a sport, so what was I thinking? – a couple of the questions I asked myself after being teased.

Because of my childhood experiences, I always felt a bit out of place in my work environments. I was overly concerned with being "too black," "not black enough," or just drawing too much attention to myself in general. To add to that, by this point in my adult life I was a tattooed, masculine of center lesbian. There were times where I could literally feel the pressure of being further marginalized within an already marginalized group by my peers, employers, and prospective employers.

To be "reduced" from a person, to a woman, to a young woman, to a young black woman, to a young black lesbian woman, to a young black masculine of center lesbian woman, to a young black masculine of center lesbian woman with tattoos felt like my place in the world was being taken away from me before I'd even had the opportunity to claim it. It became exhausting feeling like I needed to activate an invisible suit of armor before facing the world every day.

Over time I realized some of my discomfort and uncertainty was self-imposed due to my own insecurities and lack of confidence. I wasn't necessarily being treated differently in the workplace all the time, but regardless of whether I was or not, I thought I was and, even worse, I expected to be because of my past experiences.

Once I was able to get out of my own way and change my perception of my situation, my life changed. Instead of tiptoeing around trying not to make too much noise, I began leaving my mark everywhere I went. Self-reflection is not an easy thing to do, and by no means am I saying discrimination is not a real thing; it is very real. However, in my case, as easy as it was for me to fall back on any one of my diverse characteristics when things didn't go my way (which may have very well been the reason), I chose to look for other opportunities for improvement; things I could actually change.

My journey into cybersecurity did not begin with a traditional IT role, education, or certifications. I left home at the age of 17 and moved to Miami, FL where I attended the University of Miami. My major was computer engineering, and it did not take long for me to realize I'd made a mistake because I was not enjoying or connecting with what I was learning. I dropped out after the first year. Two years, a departure and return to Miami, another false start in college, and a brief period of homelessness later, things began to change for the better.

In the early 2000s, I landed a role with BellSouth as a DSL (Digital Subscriber Line) installer. At the time, DSL was considered high speed internet and dial-up modems were quickly becoming a thing of the past. My day to day was roughly 90% telecommunications and 10% computers and networking. When customers asked me how to set up Wi-Fi or share the high-speed connectivity with multiple computers, I was disappointed when I had to tell them it was outside the scope of the installation. Although it wasn't my job to provide connectivity beyond a single directly connected computer, I wanted to, at the very least, offer some guidance, but the truth was I had no idea how.

Within my first year on the job, I saved enough money to buy a few computers from the local thrift store, a router, a switch, and two books: PCs for Dummies and Networking for Dummies. I built a home lab and taught myself all about building computers and designing networks. After gaining some confidence in my abilities, I began providing IT services to businesses and residences to earn extra money. After seven years as a DSL installer, I wanted more for my career and I was ready for a change of scenery. So, I left Miami and moved to New York.

I had no formal education, one certification (CompTIA A+), and other than my side gig (which was not listed on my resume) I had no professional IT experience. After being turned down for jobs so many times I lost count, the owner of a small IT services company took a chance on me and offered me a part-time role as a junior network and systems administrator. I worked extremely hard to prove myself, and within two weeks, I was offered a full-time position. Since I wasn't officially trained or certified in any particular technology, I had to become incredibly resourceful; and fast. I was responding to issues in person at customer locations, so I was troubleshooting, researching, and answering questions all at the same time (truthfully, I was freaking out inside at times, as well).

The more I was able to find solutions and solve problems, the more confident I became. The more confident I became, the more I wanted to learn and do. I began researching education and certification opportunities, but I could not afford either. As an alternative, I built another home lab with used and recycled equipment. I used whatever free resources I could get my hands on to help me learn and expand my skillset. My passion was in networking and infrastructure; I think it's because my background in telecommunications made the concepts familiar. Building home labs and challenging myself became my hobby, and as a result, my confidence in my abilities continued to improve.

By 2011, I'd worked my way up to a leadership role as Director of IT Services at a Managed Services Provider. I was originally hired by the company (a computer repair and retail shop at the time) as a contractor to handle offsite residential and business requests on an as needed basis. Within six months, I was a fulltime employee, working with the owner to build a full-blown managed services business. I was responsible for the end-to-end design and delivery of our services offerings which mostly consisted of network and infrastructure deployment, performance monitoring, and maintenance.

At this point in my career, I was a four-time college dropout with no degree, one certification, and even though my practical experience was obtained over a period of time much longer than the previous four years, I was happy to have four years of documented, professional IT experience on my resume. I didn't know what imposter syndrome was at the time, but as I think back, the director role was definitely my first time experiencing it. There were days where I wondered why I was in the role, why the owner trusted me so much, and even why customers believed in me and trusted my recommendations. On the surface, I was an experienced professional that delivered effective IT solutions with confidence. But on the inside, I was a scared little girl waiting to be rejected or ridiculed for not have the same background or credentials as my peers (predominantly male, of course) in similar roles.

Ultimately, I decided that instead of feeling sorry for myself, I would work even harder than I had been. I started to research and build a master plan. Initially, my approach was studying job descriptions and qualifications for roles similar to mine and roles I found interesting. I noted my gaps and put a plan in place to address them. I wasn't targeting a specific role or trying to build a career plan. My goal was to become so good at my craft that I couldn't be ignored even if discrimination was at play.

Goal #1: finish my college degree. In December of 2012 I went back to college for the fifth time in pursuit of a Bachelor's Degree in Information Technology. In 2015, I became the first member of my family to earn a college degree (even picked up the CCNA certification along the way, which was goal #2). I can't begin to describe how accomplished, complete, and relieved I felt when I made it through that program. I'd finally finished something. When my diploma arrived in the mail and I held it in my hands for the first time, I was overcome by a sense of drive and purpose.

During my bachelor's program studies I decided I wanted to specialize. After researching the job market, roles, trends, etc. I narrowed my options to a choice between software development, cloud, and cybersecurity. I was never drawn to programming and I was not confident in my ability to pivot to a career in cloud and be successful (cloud was not nearly as widely adopted back then as it is now). Cybersecurity, however, seemed right up my alley based on my background, skillset, and interests. Although I was not exclusively focused on cybersecurity in my role as director, security was integrated into all aspects of the services offering.

Immediately following the completion of my bachelor's degree, I began my laser focused journey into cybersecurity by pursing a master's degree in information assurance. Over the next several years, I completed two master's degrees and a list of certifications including CISSP, C|EH, C|HFI, and ITILv3. Over the course of this three-year period, I held a couple of cybersecurity roles, and eventually joined eSentire, my current employer. I began my career as a Senior Solutions Engineer supporting the New York territory as an individual contributor and after 18 months I was promoted into my current role, leading the global solutions engineering team.

In addition to my role at eSentire, I am also an adjunct professor of Cybersecurity and course author at Yeshiva University, a football coach, and a PhD student (I am currently pursuing a PhD in Organizational Leadership). My wife and I have been together for a little over five years and married for three and a half. We have two sons, two dogs, and a wonderful support system.

I am now viewed as a thought leader and an expert in the field. I was recognized by SC Media as a 2019 Reboot Leadership Award recipient in the Outstanding Educator category, as well as The Software Report's Top 25 Women Leaders in Cybersecurity and Cyber Defense Magazine's Top 100 Women in Cybersecurity: both in 2020. The awards gave me pause initially because I never do anything for recognition. I am simply a driven, passionate professional with a high degree of integrity and a strong work ethic. What I came to realize, however, is that I could use my platform to bring visibility to others by speaking on behalf of those who need a voice; the underrepresented and marginalized groups of individuals in tech who need to feel empowered, represented, and encouraged.

I did not have a mentor to guide me or help me navigate my career. In fact, my first time ever having a mentor was after I was nearly 20 years into my career. Although forging my own path taught me to be resilient, determined, and confident, the road was long, lonely, and hard. Prior to having a mentor, I found my way through lots of trial and error, false starts, setbacks, and headaches.

I lost a lot of time, wasted a lot of money, and missed out on a number of opportunities. Despite my tribulations, I remained dedicated and steadfast in my pursuits and now I am at a point in my career where I believe my journey, my story and my experiences can help others.

In October 2020 I founded Empow(H)er Cybersecurity, a non-profit organization aimed at empowering women of color to pursue and have successful cybersecurity careers. From the time we're born, far too many women of color see our growth potential stunted and our curiosity discouraged. We encounter glass ceilings and, often, are denied one of the most basic human rights — the freedom to find one's self. Rather than letting us become who we are, we're told who we should be, what we should love and, in many instances, which field to pursue. For women of color, a career path in cybersecurity isn't often presented as viable or realistic. And it's not because we don't have the potential to fall in love with or excel in the field, it's most often due to a lack of exposure. Empow(H)er Cybersecurity provides a safe space for women of color interested in a career in cybersecurity to learn from and be encouraged and inspired by other women of color who have found success in the field.

I also mentor outside my non-profit organization in an effort broaden my reach and positively impact as many lives as possible. During my conversations with mentees, I often share things I learned along the way, the hard way. I've included a few of them below.

- "Success lies just outside the area where comfort dwells." – The idea here is to get comfortable with being uncomfortable. If we are not uncomfortable, we are not learning and growing. Don't be afraid to challenge yourself and stretch yourself beyond the things you know you do well. Learn something new. Try something scary.

- "Failure is not permanent." – My philosophy is, I never fail. I either succeed or I learn. It's important to remind yourself that the only way failure becomes permanent is if you stop trying. If we change our mind or perception, we change our world. Look at failures as opportunities - stepping stones on the path to success. Failure is necessary. Embrace it, expect it, but don't let it stick around for too long.
- "Celebrate every win." – No matter how big or small, every win is part of your story, you earned it, and you should pat yourself on the back for it. Don't be so focused on the end goal that you ignore the milestones. They are important as well.
- Know your why. – Why do you want to pursue a career in cybersecurity? What are your desired outcomes? Why did you choose the path you're on? Having these answers and standing firm in them will help you remain grounded when the road gets tough; and it will get tough.
- Know your worth. – Be prepared to differentiate yourself. How are you unique when compared to other individuals with the same qualifications and skills as you? What's your value add? What is it about you that will make others remember your name?

When young girls and women hear my story or witness my journey and the things I've overcome, I want them to see where I am today and know for themselves with an extremely high degree of confidence that they can do it as well. I want others to feel empowered by my successes, my failures, and my lessons learned. The mind is incredibly powerful. We are exactly who we think we are, and we can achieve whatever we believe we can achieve. Whether a person's mentality continues to move them forward or hold them back is the question. I've been on both sides of that mental coin, and what I represent today (and will continue to represent) is the decision to never give up always push forward; just like my mom did time and time again.

Even though I have found my way to success, I refuse to let myself get too comfortable. Whether for myself, my family, my friends, or my employer, every day, I strive to be better in some way than the day before. Every day is an opportunity to learn and grow and I am a believer in taking full advantage of the opportunities I am presented with. I hope that being true to myself and going after the things I want in life sets a positive example for others and inspires them to do the same.

Chapter 7

Name: Vina Ta

Job Title: SOC Analyst II

Company: Binary Defense

Location: North Canton, Ohio, USA

The Set Path

Ever since I was little, I always thought that I was going to be a teacher; I was transitioning from a junior to senior in college for middle childhood education specializing in math and science. It was a set path, I always thought that I was going to be a teacher, it was what I was meant to be. I even got a part-time job while going to college at Mad Science. It is where I did after school enrichment programs, special events, and birthday parties to teach kids science and have them have a greater appreciation for science. Everyone I knew said that I was meant to be a teacher because of my personality and the way I understand children.

It is important to remember that just because you have a set path does not mean that it is the only way for you to travel. Sometimes you must risk it, try something new and venture out o your comfort zone. You never know where life is going to take you, you never know who you are going to meet that might change your life for better or worse. It is important to question and think about what is best for you. Is it better to go down a defined path that is set for you or to venture into something new and scary?

The Inspiration

Little did I know everything was going to change in my life when I started working for a department at my college. I guess for me things really changed when I made friends with a guy who worked across from me, he always seemed so happy and excited to be on his laptop whenever it was slow. Then one day I asked him what he was working on, he told me "I am creating a website for my web programming class." I half-jokingly told him that it sounded interesting and that I am going to make that my minor. He laughed and said, "Sure you are."

You never know what's going to inspire you, for me it was seeing the passion my friend had when he was creating a website for a school project. It was how proud he felt showing me his project that he had worked so hard on. This was what really inspired me to want to get into computer science. I was honestly very afraid that I wouldn't be able to learn programming. I had enjoyed education, but something inside me felt missing.

The Addition

Something in me told me that I should be looking for more, I thought about the idea of getting my minor in computer science all weekend long. I thought that it would give me the edge over other future teachers being able to teach technology.

I decided to talk with my guidance counselor that Monday. I told him that I would like to make computer science my minor. The way he looked at me when I told him, you would've thought I was crazy, especially since I was so close to graduating. Although, he did tell me that was a good minor to get because everything involves technology and that it would only add an extra semester.

Afterwards, I had told that friend I had officially made computer science my minor and that I would be starting that adventure next semester. He seems to be in as much disbelief as my guidance counselor.

Later, I told my friends and family that I was making computer science as my minor and my graduation date would be pushed back a semester. They did not originally support me, nevertheless, I persisted through the negativity and mostly confusion I was getting from my family and peers.

The Start of Something New

Fast forward to me being in my first computer science class, the first day was a struggle, but I did learn how to cout "Hello World!" in C++. I had originally thought that this class was going to teach me the history of computers and how it worked. I was very wrong; we were learning how to program in the C++ programming language. Everything in that class felt so new and foreign to me like learning a new language.

At the end of my class, I told Dr. Guerico I do not think this is the right fit for me, I do not know what I am doing in this classroom full of men. (This was my first experience with imposter syndrome and not feeling like I belong in this classroom) I was going from a class with the majority being females to primarily men. The other woman in my class was just there for her math major requirement.

She really believed in me when most of the people around me said I could not do it and that I would drop out of the major or go back to education. She saw my potential and gave me the courage I needed to stay when everyone else said I should just give up. She told me to give it a semester and to attend a Women in Tech conference.

At the conference, I was really inspired by the women speakers and how they gave back to the community through mentorship and events to inspire girls & women alike. It really helped me to see that computer science could be a path for me. I finally understood what impostor syndrome was, it's when you feel like you do not belong to something even though you have the qualifications to perform it. In a field dominated by men, it's OK to be a woman. It wasn't going to be an easy road, but it would be a road worth traveling. Well, a semester turned into me switching from a major in education to Bachelor of Arts in computer science.

The Computer Science Group

I ended up making good friends with an excellent group of guys who were also in my computer science classes. They have been with me since the beginning of my journey, most of them were/had switched to computer science as well. Yet in the back of my mind, I still felt like I did not belong mostly because the guys were learning at a much quicker pace than me. I think it is important to understand that who you become friends with is important. We helped push and motivate each other to graduate. There was only one person from the group who did not graduate but decided to enlist in the marines instead.

We always saw the best in each other, we did not give up when things got tough, we just studied harder and asked each other questions when one of us did not understand what the professors were telling us. They are honestly great guys that did not treat me differently just because I was a woman. Looking back, I am so lucky that I have been surrounded by good men who saw me as an equal and treat me as an individual, for that I will always be thankful for them because they set the bar for how I want to be treated by men at a workplace.

The Enhanced Major

I had originally planned to just get my Bachelor of Arts in computer science because it was the quickest path to getting a degree. I realized that programming wasn't something I really wanted to pursue but I was close to graduating. I was talking to my friends after what appeared to be a successful interview and hopefully a potential job in the field.

My friend said something that changed my path indefinitely soon after. He essentially said, if you don't get the job, it's much better to get the Bachelor of Sciences, not an art. It shows that you took the harder path with more advanced math and computer science classes. Also, it looks so much better to recruiters and potential managers.

I ended up not getting the job, someone who worked for that company got it instead of me, so I decided to listen to him to get my Bachelor of Science. It was exceedingly difficult switching to a harder Bachelors of Science, mostly because I had to take calculus II when the last time I took calculus was three and a half years ago. I felt like if I would have graduated with a Bachelor Arts, I really would not have had a stronger foundation, furthermore, I would not have found my true path to cyber security.

The Woman in Cyber Security

decided to apply for an internship the very first day of January. I heard back from the recruiter within a couple of days, she told me that there was a lady who was interested in hiring me but for a different position than what I applied to. The position was being a business security intern, but with a big focus on education, awareness, and training. This was the perfect blend of my educational background and my new understanding of cyber security. It was at this internship that I learned that I wanted to be in the cyber security field.

My manager, Lauren Zink showed me what a woman can do in cyber security. She is an industry recognized and awarded security awareness and engagement manager. You can read her story in volume 1. She was always good at giving feedback and making sure my voice was heard. We worked as a team when we did projects, she never made me feel left out. She showed me what I can potentially do in cyber security. Just when I felt like I belonged, things decided to twist and turn. As fate would have it, she moved to a different company, so I had to work for the director of cyber security instead.

It was at this internship that I learned that nothing ever stays the same for long, that change is always going to happen. They had two very distinct types of personality and style of management, I learned that I had to become like a chameleon. I do not change who I am but adapt to the distinct types of personalities that are within a company, so that I can get the best results out of people when working.

At the same time, my school had just added a new professor and a new concentration for computer science, cybersecurity. I realized as I started the semester that this was going to be my path, not programming or being a software developer. Dr. Chae really inspired me to get into cyber security. He was genuinely so passionate about what he taught. He showed us the potential different paths that someone could do in this field.

The Reassurance

ended up going to a career and internship fair and talking with two directors of a company; they asked me if I was looking for an internship in information technology. I straightforwardly told them I wanted to work in cyber security not become a business intelligence, programmer, or software developer. (I learned that it is important to stay true to yourself and what you really want to do and not settle for anything less than what you deserve.) They told me that their security team was just getting started and that they would take my resume to the recruiter and the director of cybersecurity and see where it goes from here.

The company created an internship just for me and added a Women in STEM (science, technology, engineering, and math) initiative with women leaders from the company. It really sharpens my overall cyber security skills interning at this place.

My manager Andy, he was truly kind, joyful, and always made sure my voice was heard in a meeting. I was lucky to have a manager who cared about me and believed in my work. He always included me and made me feel like I belonged in the team, but like all good things this internship ended around the same time that I graduated.

The Job Hunting

Job hunting is never fun, I applied to so many different companies and various positions in cyber security. It is especially important to never give up when you're job searching. I realized at the various interviews that it is not just them interviewing you to see if you fit the company, but also to see if you feel like you fit in with the company environment.

Sometimes the best places to get a potential job interview is at a career fair or at a tech/security conference. it is important to make a good first impression, build the connections and add them to your network. You never know who they will become. I made a friend at one of my internships; he was originally a contractor and now he's the director of cybersecurity for that company.

Eventually, I applied for a position that is now where I work. I did not hear back from Binary Defense for about a week and a half, at the same time I was talking to a recruiter for the United States military. He was telling me about different opportunities and paths with my degree. We were close to me signing the papers, when Binary Defense sent me a message saying that I got the job!

It's important to remember that sometimes it takes a job a little while for them to reach out to you and not to give up hope especially when something felt right at the interview. Don't forget to send them a thank you letter for taking time out of their day to schedule an interview with you.

The Imposter Syndrome Disappeared

It was an unbelievable experience to finally start my career in the industry. It is where I belong, my impostor syndrome faded once I got this job. My family was happy for me and they told all their friends and family. They were not prepared for me to switch majors suddenly, but now they know this is my path and they are proud of how far I have come.

In Vietnamese culture, nine is a very lucky number, my start date was September 9th, 2019 at 9:00 AM. It honestly didn't feel real until I started my job as a SOC Analyst II, but I've been working here for over a year and half now. As a SOC analyst, our primary job is to monitor SIEMs (security information event manager) and our very own MDR (managed detection and response) solution. Essentially, we are the first line of defense against cyber-attacks and threats by alerting clients about anything suspicious or unusual in their environment 24/7/365. We always have analysts watching making sure our clients are protected and alerted if something suspicious pops up at any given moment.

I am so happy that my job sees me as a person and not as a number. That my manager is informative, supportive and gives the best constructive feedback, so you can grow into the best version of yourself. The team I work with are all good people who care about what they do and the people they work with.

The COVID-19 and My Mental Health

Everything went smoothly and the men I worked with on shift are all great guys, then things changed with COVID-19. I had developed anxiety for the first time in my life because originally the coronavirus was connected to China. Then I saw the news that Asian American people were getting harassed and hurt because of it. I was so scared to leave the house and be with people. I'm usually such a people person that I was feeling heartbroken and sad that people were judging you solely based on your appearance instead of your character. Eventually as time went on, I went outside (safely and at a distance) and people were nice to me and things started to go back to a better state mentally for me.

I also learned that it's important to have a good mental health, it affects how you perform at work. Working from home is usually a luxury for most people, but I'm not one of them for I am a people person. There are ways to help with that feeling of being alone such as listening music, having a good routine, being grateful for still having a job. I even started to refocus and reignite my passion for cyber security by working harder and studying for my security plus certification.

The Future

My first step in getting certified, to prove to myself that I do know and understand the basics of cybersecurity. I want to eventually be working more directly with others or be like my manager Lauren Zink. My goal one day is to build a foundation or start a chapter for women and girls in technology more specifically cyber security. A place where women and girls feel safe, and their voices heard. Where you can express your passion for cyber security and/or technology.

The Summary

My path to cybersecurity started with watching someone being passionate about web programming. Ironically, I never liked web programming once I was in my major. Then I went to women in tech conferences and saw that I was not alone in how I felt. It made me feel good knowing that others experienced something like me. My group of friends I made in college inspired me to push further than I thought I could do myself. At my internships, I knew that cyber security was my path and was not going to settle for anything less.

Remember your path is never set in stone and that it is never too late to chase your dreams.

Chapter 8

Name: Federica Vitale

Job Title: Compliance, Risk and Data Privacy Associate

Company: NCTech Ltd

Location: Edinburgh, UK

"Three magical ingredients that led me to become one of the youngest international privacy professionals: passion, persistence and knowledge."

"You are going to be an excellent lawyer, Federica."

This is certainly one of the most recurrent quotes that immediately comes to my mind and that some of the closest people in my life have said to me at least once when I accomplished something important. It fills my heart to receive these kind of compliments and while I work towards becoming the lawyer I want to be, I like to do my part in sustaining and empowering all the incredible women that I meet along the way. I sincerely hope that my story will somehow inspire you and that it will lead you to reach the most beautiful goals you have in your personal life plan.

I am a 26-year-old Italian woman who loves the legal field more than anything else in this world. What fascinates me most about law is not only its technicality, its overall objective in achieving the common good, but also the way it teaches you to look at the reality you live in. I do not know if I was simply supposed to take this path because of the way I am but what I do know is that there have been life events that have led me to become the person I am today and that have led me to choose the legal sector with a twist of information technology law.

I was born in the city of Turin in Italy; here I lived until the age of twelve. When I think back about my childhood, the picture of a playful, energetic, friendly, and proactive young girl with a happy family immediately comes up in my mind. It is surely thanks to both my parent that I am who I am. Both of them have contributed in a different way to my personal growth but my curiosity for what lies outside home probably started with my mother's life background. Since she was born in Italy but grew up in Germany she has always been deeply passionate about the German culture, which I got the chance to experience when we used to go on road trips to visit my grandparents.

During primary school, I developed an interest in foreign languages and English, in particular. My parents have always told me that I was one of my English teacher's favourite students because I always used to raise my hand in class and studied new words very passionately. It was this passion that led me to win an English language competition, which allowed students in primary school to go on a trip to Oxford University, England, United Kingdom (UK). I do not think I was a genius, but I am definitely passionate about foreign languages and my passions have always pushed me to reach my goals no matter what.

My passion for foreign languages continued throughout high school, where I became more aware of my global citizenship. It was at this point of my life that I started embracing the spirit of a socially and politically aware citizen who can start making changes by contributing to the local community. This is because, by studying foreign languages, I was given the chance to learn about other cultures and to have a better understanding of international cooperation. I still remember going to conferences after school on topics around the future of Democracy and diplomatic relations affecting the social changes of that time. It was during my teenage years that I became fascinated by the beauty of diversity that surrounded me and by the unfamiliarity of what stands outside my comfort zone. In other words, that young girl who my parents have always described as independent and obstinate, became the young girl who wanted to see the world while leaning towards what is unconventional.

When the time came to go to University, my intention on which course I wanted to start was clear. I wanted to study law and become a lawyer, and, at the same time, I wanted to work in an area of law that would have allowed me to travel or at least that would combine different jurisdictions all together. This is because I like the interaction between different legal systems, and I like to see how solutions are found with the contribution of different minds. At the beginning of my legal journey, however, I was not entirely sure about which area of law would combine all my interests. I am passionate about intellectual property, criminal justice and I have always wanted to contribute to the society as much as I possibly can but, initially, I was on a personal mission looking for the perfect niche. That is to say it is entirely normal not to know sometimes what we actually want but, as human beings, we can always find our own paths by keeping our interests alive and by investing time in them.

One of the main turning points in my life was when I started taking part in a variety of Models of United Nations, simulations run by international students from any study field aimed at forming the future global leaders. They represent a way for young leaders around the world to contribute to the current global issues we face as an international community but also to become better citizens of tomorrow. These experiences, in particular, gave me not only the chance to interact with students from every corner of the world but also to realise how much I still had to learn and how far I should have gone in order to reach my goals. It was after my initial experiences that I realised I was ready to leave my national borders to see what else was awaiting me. It is thanks to Models of United Nations, therefore, that I have learnt not to be scared of taking on a new challenge and the importance of empowering others in order to see a change.

I have always wanted to make the most out of my studies in order to learn continuously and achieve my dreams. As the first woman in my family's generation to obtain a degree, I have always wanted to make an impact and provide possible solutions by putting into practice one of the most powerful tools an individual can have, knowledge. After moving to the United Kingdom, I started acquiring a variety of skills such as leadership, public speaking, team working and management. During law school, I got the opportunity to be in charge of a Legal Clinic as its Director and to provide free legal advice to members of the public who could not afford a solicitor while also coordinating a team of more than seventy volunteers. This invaluable and life changing experience gave me the chance to advise on a variety of legal cases as well as the tools to deal with what I do now on a daily basis. It taught me how to deal with confidential information, how to handle a case, how to interact with a client and how to deal with more than one task at a time.

Personal journeys, however, are made of highs and lows. I would not be telling the whole truth if I told you just about whatever went right. Despite my braveness and my continuous focus on my career, I did have moments in which I felt lonely and, why not, sometimes lost. I think it is normal that while we are discovering new aspects of ourselves or new interests we do not know whether we are doing the right thing, but it is always worth trying to see if it works out for ourselves. It is possible that we have our 'own moments' that nobody else can understand but talking with the people around us will always help. I have never had anyone in my family who could assist me with my applications in order to succeed and obtain legal work experience, for example. I have always had to figure that out myself and I have managed to do so until today not only because of the genuine drive I have that guides me in my choices but also because I have always learnt something new from whoever came into my life. Getting into the legal world is not easy but finding mentors and being open to receive constructive criticism will always benefit you.

One of the biggest challenges I have faced is being a recent law graduate in the middle of a global health crisis. This is because working for years and years to get as much work experience as possible and then finding yourself in a moment of a global unprecedented uncertainty, is not something easy to handle. After my graduation, I lived moments in which I felt completely lost. I was seeing the major news talking about the many lives the global pandemic was taking away, I was seeing the economy worsening and the unemployment rate increasing. In similar circumstances, it was probably like standing on a podium with a trophy in your hands in the middle of the desert. You have nowhere to go and nothing to do with what you have just achieved. However, it is exactly in those moments we realise the importance of what we already have, the importance of our health and of those we love and how important it is to never quit from working on our goals. After all, the world has moved online and as human beings, we adapt quickly to the change. This is why it is important to be proactive and to focus on the positive side of whatever happens around us. In doing so, we might often be able to find all the answers to our questions.

have never wanted to give up my goals and so I had to find a solution. Despite the pandemic, I saw firms and companies were offering the chance to have virtual experiences and, as a passionate individual, I immediately took the chance to get involved as much as I could. I still remember some of the rejections that I got during my law school years to have physical work experience in a variety of offices during the summer but this time it was going differently. In such a similar uncertain time, I was actually obtaining positive responses to my applications. I got selected as one of the 2020 Summer Scholars for HP, an experience that improved my knowledge of the technology sector and in the factors that affect a business choice. I got the opportunity to work on a virtual business project with other legal professionals and I became a Legal Advisor for an educational NGO that empowers students from around the world through virtual internships. All of these experiences were certainly different, and they were all missing that human interaction we are just so used to have in our everyday lives but, at the same time, they were teaching me new skills. Despite the remote nature of those experiences, it was then that I realised I have always been passionate about technology and that thanks to it I could combine all my interests under the same roof. By understanding the problems affecting businesses, I developed an interest in data protection and privacy law, which have become of crucial importance in a similar virtual environment. I therefore started to look for work positions that could potentially allow me to work in this interesting sector. There was only one problem, all the different positions I was looking at were requiring candidates to have years and years of experience and I was just a recent graduate. To be specific, I was a recent graduate in the middle of a global pandemic.

While thinking back to those moments, I remember that there were days that I thought 'you are in the middle of a pandemic where people are losing their jobs, why would you make it?.' At first, it seemed like an impossible mission. After all, if a company wanted to hire someone it is obvious that they would prefer someone with years of experience. This is because companies have shifted from working in their offices to working remotely and so the on-boarding process of a new candidate is certainly easier if that candidate already knows what to do. On the other hand, I have always been persistent and improving my abilities has always been important to me. I wanted to try and by applying for jobs and undergoing some interviews, I ultimately obtained the job I currently have as a Compliance, Risk and Data Privacy Associate.

As a recent graduate, I am probably one of the youngest among all the other privacy professionals, but this has never intimidated me. I have always loved learning from others, and I think that everyone has something to offer. During my interviews, I thought that the only way I could break the barrier of some requirements was by allowing employers to get to know me and how committed I am to do whatever is necessary to contribute. I do not think there is a specific way that will ultimately always lead you to be successful at interviews. The only thing you can do is be yourself so that the employers in front of you can have a better understanding of your abilities, goals, values and see whether they can place their trust in you. At my job interview, for example, I talked about all the roles of responsibility I held during my studies but also about the abilities that I learnt from those experiences which could potentially help the company in achieving its business goals. I really wanted the position I currently hold with all my heart, not only because it was a way of combining my interests but also because of the international reach that the company has, and which would have allowed me to deal with different jurisdictions. It was by sharing my ambitious career plan that I obtained the trust of my current employer. I still remember that at my third interview for the same position, the person who recruited me started the conversation by talking about the years of experience that other candidates had compared to mine. It was during those minutes that my initial thoughts were 'alright, you have not made it and that is because you do not have enough years of experience for this role'. However, immediately after that brief introduction, I was told that my values and the person seen at the different stages of the interviews reflected a lot of the values of the company itself and that therefore they were happy to welcome me into the team. It was in that exact and very exciting moment that I realised that there will always be people out there ready to believe in you and invest in your potential.

As a Compliance, Risk and Data Privacy Associate, I get the chance to deal with a variety of duties. My main role is to make sure the company complies with all the different requirements that must be in place in relation to privacy and data protection law but also to ensure global compliance depending on where the business activity is being carried out. Thanks to this role, I constantly have the chance to deal with legislative changes and updates on data protection law and to liaise with a variety of privacy and cyber security professionals. My duties go from working closely with the Data Protection Officer while ensuring compliance with the General Data Protection Regulation (GDPR), the UK Data Protection Act 2018 and other international pieces of legislation in relation to privacy, to working on policies that aim at preventing potential data breaches. I always have the chance to review Privacy Policies, Cookie policies, contracts' terms and conditions and to deal with data subjects' requests. This allows me to belong to the very wide and international family of privacy and cyber security professionals.

From the first moment I started working as a Compliance, Risk and Data Privacy Associate, I understood how valuable data is and how important it is to have protective measures in place. Although we have always had our personal data online and expected some level of privacy, I believe the pandemic has certainly changed the way individuals see their privacy now. People are becoming more and more aware of their rights and freedoms in relation to their privacy and expect their data to be protected by companies. Surveillance is always a constant whenever we access an IoT product; continuous awareness of individuals has placed data protection in a leading position across the board. While data protection law continues to evolve around the world alongside the different improvements in technology, prevention, transparency, prompt incident response will still be the key. It is undeniable that the transborder data flows will increase in the years to come as well as the proliferation of malware and hacking activities in cyberspace. In order to mitigate these risks promptly, there will always be privacy professionals ready to help as guardians of data.

To conclude, my best advice for someone who wants to start a new career is never stop learning from others but, at the same time, never stop believing in your potential. These two ingredients combined with passion and interest will certainly guide you wherever you want to go. As human beings, it is quite normal not always to know what we want but investing our

...me and energies on what we like will surely reveal the answers we are looking for. Finding ...entors who share their opinions with you and support you in your projects is certainly ...other key ingredient. One of the most empowering things one of my mentors told me is that ...is normal to have setbacks, but these happen on our way to motivate us even more and that ...why "the sky can only be your starting point." As women, we might not only encounter the ...neral difficulties of finding jobs during an uncertain historical moment, but we might also ...ce some stereotypes. It is exactly in those moments that we must push forward to break the ...rriers of those stereotypes by believing in ourselves and in all the beautiful abilities we can ...ing along. Justice Ruth Bader Ginsburg, a woman I have constantly found to be ...spirational, has taught me that.

*...would like to be remembered as someone who used whatever talent she had to do her work
the very best of her ability."*

...s a young privacy professional, I still have a long way to go but I do believe that every day ...a lesson and that nobody should ever be able to stop you from achieving your dreams.

Chapter 9

Name: Gyle dela Cruz

Job title: Cyber Threat Analyst

Company: Cyber Research New Zealand

Location: Melbourne, Australia

Shouldn't Have

In the past two years, I've come to realise that there have been a lot of 'shouldn't have's in my life. I was the baby who shouldn't have survived, if not for the miraculous invention called the incubator where I was left for a few weeks after my mother was discharged from the government hospital. I had respiratory ailments when I was a toddler and shouldn't have survived, if not for the loving care of my father, who took me to Manila Bay daily back when it wasn't very polluted, for the morning sea breeze. This was the cheaper folk remedy that was supposed to help kids overcome their childhood asthma issues.

You see, I grew up in a country where a dictator and his family and cronies lived luxurious lives while the majority of citizens were dirt poor. I am too young to remember this family story, but my dad would often tell us the reason why he decided to find work overseas. My mother almost died from a gastro-intestinal disease, because he couldn't afford to take her to the hospital. It was agonizing for him to see his wife becoming delirious while his three young daughters looked from the bedroom doorway, crying because their mother was in pain. It was only my paternal grandmother's knowledge of local herbal remedies that helped my mother survive that fateful night. It took my father years before he got an offer from an overseas job placement agency. During the era before LinkedIn and online job platforms, the only way a job seeker from a third world country could find a job in the Middle East was to apply to overseas job placement agencies. It was a gamble, because one had to pay the local placement fee and hope the agency had legitimate contacts with employers in the more affluent countries and didn't abscond with the placement fees.

When I was in third grade, my father gave me his first heart-to-heart talk. He said he needed to go abroad so he could give us a decent future, by which he meant being able to send us to college. He didn't want us to incur debts, and knew it was difficult to be a working student. He and my mother met in college when they were both working full time jobs and studying at night. As the eldest daughter, he told me, I needed to set a good example for my younger sisters now that he was going to be away for years; I needed to help my mother take care of everyone. Mom worked full time and my paternal grandmother took care of us when we got home from school. The outcome of that talk gave me the confidence that I could be entrusted with serious responsibilities.

I've always been the serious one because I was the big sister not just to my biological sisters, but also to the rest of the kids in the neighborhood. The bullies steered clear of me after I showed them that they couldn't get away with pushing and hurting my younger sisters. It has been decades, but I remember that warm day during the dry season when we were playing outside and a boy known for being mean and spoiled pushed my sister away for no good reason at all, and she fell to the ground. I asked the boy to apologise and never do that again. He responded that he could do anything he wanted and started to run around trying to push other kids away. I've never been athletic. I shouldn't have been able to do it but that time, I rushed after him until I caught him by his hair. All I remember was telling him to never ever hurt my sister or anyone again in the neighborhood, while he kept clawing at my hand which I moved away from his. He eventually got away and ran back home while I was left clutching some of his hair. My friends told me they were surprised to see me move so fast, and that I was incredibly strong because I was able to shake that boy as if he were a rag doll even though I was only three inches taller than he. He was grounded when all the kids told his mom what he had done and for the rest of that dry season, his mom made sure that his head was shaved.

So, I grew up without a father. I didn't know that his contract only stipulated one free trip home every two years. We kept asking our mother when will Dad get home, and the answer was "Once his contract says so." The first Christmas without him was painful, but I learned to deal with it because I knew we needed to be practical. I focused on my academic studies. I also read a lot of novels; I frequently had a dictionary by my side so I could look up the meaning of words. English was my second language, and I vowed at the young age of nine that one day I'd be able to speak English well enough that a native English speaker would be able to understand what I was saying. It was around that time that I got my school library card. That card opened a whole new world to me. Instead of feeling lonely and sad when my dad was so far away, I immersed myself in the worlds dreamt of and created by authors. I taught myself to speed read because I wanted to read as many books as I could during the school year. Oh yes, I was a little nerd.

My parents worked hard to send us to a private Catholic school. But I realized, during my final year in the elementary level (before going to high school), that the Catholic school didn't really provide a good science training. I used to sneak into the high school area to take a look at the labs. I always wanted to use the microscope. I saw that the ratio was five to six students per microscope. I told my mom I wanted to learn more about science. She told me that we didn't have the money to send me to more expensive schools (called 'exclusive schools' back in the old country).

A few weeks later, she told me she had asked around and found that there were special public schools called science high schools, which provided a good science-based curriculum.

She bought a reviewer which contained sample questions, and I practised really hard. I took the entrance exam to the country's national science high school, and after I got out of the exam room, my mom asked me how I felt about the exam. I said I wasn't sure if I would pass. I explained that there were math questions involving an unusual symbol I had never seen before. She asked me to draw it. She was surprised that I didn't know what pi (π) was. It was never covered in the simple math classes in the Catholic school she'd sent us to. I felt the curriculum in that school was more religious than secular. Never to be defeated, my mom looked for a math tutor for me. When I tried again for another science high school (which was run by the city government), I passed and got in. I had to do a lot of catching up because my mathematical skills were not up to par.

When I was a freshman in high school, every day was very difficult because I was commuting to another city and there was a lot of schoolwork. I also felt that everybody around me was very competitive. I studied because I wanted to learn. I have never been good at rote memorization, and those who were good with it always had the highest grades. I almost dropped out, but I reminded myself that I wanted a more intellectually challenging and science-based curriculum. I knew that I had to work really hard because at the end of the freshman school year, we were ranked based on our grade point average and those who didn't make the mark were asked to move to other schools. Those who made the cut were grouped into sections with the first group being composed of the students with the highest-grade point average. They went to the first section, called Curie. The second section was called Darwin, the third section was called Edison and the fourth called Einstein and so on. I found it cool that the group or section names were famous scientists' names. This whittling down happened every year and for a lot of my cohorts, the ultimate goal was to get into the Curie section.

I eventually found my academic pace and, through trial and error, found my crowd. Even in a school full of nerds, there was a social hierarchy based on your section. I was still an outsider but eventually in senior year, I became the Science Club president while one of my friends became the Research Club president. My friends and I were all from the section Darwin. Those who were on the top of the school social hierarchy (in the section Curie) couldn't believe that we got those highly sought after extra-curricular club roles. I heard through the grapevine that I shouldn't have been the Science Club president because I wasn't from the Curie section. I understood how it felt to be an outsider and never cared about the social hierarchy. In doing so, I got to befriend students from the lower years. When it was time for the club elections, the lower year representatives all voted for me.

When it was time to go to university, my parents wanted me to choose computer science as a major because they said it sounded more practical. They heard about the need for more programmers. I was more interested in psychology because I wanted to understand myself better. I had several depressive episodes in high school. I shouldn't have survived those dark days, but I did and then I wanted to understand human behavior. I structured my college applications so that I had psychology as my college major choice for my dream university, while for the other applications, I put in computer science. I got accepted and offered scholarships for the computer science college applications, but I waited for my dream university. I got in and went for the BS in Psychology program, with the intention to later use this as my pre-med course. Halfway through the program, I realized that I was more interested in legal studies and shifted to the BA in Psychology program. I finished my psychology degree and applied to law school. I spent two years in law school and dropped out.

It was the most excruciatingly difficult decision I had ever made. I should have been either the first doctor or lawyer in my family. I had let my parents down.

I was in limbo after I got out of law school. Fortunately, I got connected to the Internet and once more I found a different world to explore. That's when I realized that I wanted to be part of this exciting field. At that time, there were massive recruitment drives for COBOL programmers to solve the Y2K bug issue. However, I was too late to jump onto that bandwagon. I went back to school but this time, I went for a master's degree in Information Technology. I loved the classes, but I never got to finish the program because I couldn't find a suitable topic for my research proposal. I finished all the coursework – both the courses in the program and the extra bridge courses for those without a computer science undergraduate degree. Years later, I found out that if I had just written the research proposal and kept submitting it, I would have made it. I was part of the first cohort in the program and had no one to ask for guidance. Those who came in after me had better guidance. I promised myself that I would go back to graduate school and finish a master's degree. This is also the main reason why I now volunteer as a mentor to help others who are about to start their tech or infosec career journeys, having valuable piece of advice for someone starting out is always important in helping them decide on their own paths.

While in graduate school, I also took some practical classes at a trade school, where I learned to solder in a basic electronics class. I wanted to learn how to put together desktop computers, and the only path was to go to a basic electronics class and then computer electronics until I got into the hardware parts and servicing. From this path, I was able to get to the Cisco Networking Academy program. This led to getting a free CCNA (Cisco Certified Networking Academy) voucher.

This first IT certification opened the door for me. I had difficulty finding a job in tech because I didn't have a degree in computer science. I also didn't get to finish my master's degree. I also had interviewers telling me that I was overqualified because I'd gone to graduate school! It was difficult to shift to tech. I never gave up and eventually the CCNA helped me land my first full-time IT job as a technical support engineer.

Even before I got my first tech job, I wanted to focus on security. This was because when I first got connected to the internet, I found different online communities while chatting in IRC. I also had my first online stalker there. If it wasn't for the other kind members of the communities there, I shouldn't have been able to shift to tech. I would have just disconnected and left the online world. Those friends I made in different IRC channels made sure that they watched out for that online stalker and taught me the commands to find out his IP address. I was also able to figure out his schedule and patterns based on the information shared by my chat pals there. One of the reasons why I migrated to Australia was the Aussies who helped me in the IRC channels. They were a bunch of helpful people who were welcoming and patient with a young woman's questions.

It took me some time before I was finally able to focus on cyber security. When I started out in tech, when one talked of security, it was in the context of network security like firewalls and VPNs (Virtual Private Networks). Once I figured out what I wanted to focus on, I embarked on a long process of studying DFIR (Digital Forensics and Incident Response). I read some books until I got the chance to go for my first SANS digital forensics course. I was hooked. Ever since I was a kid, I'd loved reading mystery novels and figuring out who did the crime. I also realized that I had a strong protective instinct. I also like doing analytical work. So, it made sense that I focused on this area of cyber security. I eventually got to finish my Graduate Certificate in Incident Response from the SANS Institute.

Then I used that as a way to get to graduate school. In December 2019, before the pandemic started, I completed my Master's in Cyber Security – Digital Forensics degree. The graduate program was supposed to be year-long for a full-time student. However, I was working full time and could only study part time. It took me three years to finish as a result. I never thought I would finish it because there were challenges at work that affected both my physical and mental health. I almost dropped out of the cyber security industry due to burnout. It also didn't help that my previous workplace had become increasingly hostile. Despite – or because of – the challenges, I became mentally stronger and more resilient. I've always valued my personal integrity and have not been afraid to speak truth to power.

My shift to tech has been full of sacrifices. I saved up to pay for my classes, borrowed books and had part-time jobs. When I finally got a job in tech, I encountered misogyny and discrimination because of my gender and my skin color. This is why I work harder and make sure that my work speaks for itself. I've experienced situations when it was perfectly all right for a man to say he didn't know but when I said the same thing, I was mocked. I also had several experiences when I was always being second-guessed or I had my ideas only accepted if a man said it or supported it after I voiced it out. I've also been at the end of several mansplaining situations. I've learned to stand up for myself and call out disrespectful behavior. Sometimes it worked, sometimes it didn't. I've learnt that it is important to find allies, champions, and mentors. Now, I prioritize my well-being and if the environment is toxic, I figure out a way to find a better environment. Life is too short to be in a bad vironment. Of course, I also had to be practical. Sometimes, I can't just rage-quit because ere are bills to pay and I need to be patient.

2019, I was fortunate to be accepted into the first cohort of the Project Friedman. This was project by the Australian Women in Security Network (AWSN) and WomenSpeakCyber to lp more women speak at conferences. I've always wanted to share my knowledge, but I uldn't figure out how I could get to speak at conferences or do public speaking. It also lped that the BSides Melbourne conference started in 2019 and they offered great resources r CFPs (Call for Presentations) which I eagerly devoured. Through the coaching and entorship opportunities I got that year, I was finally able to find my voice. In 2020, I allenged myself to speak at a conference or do a presentation twice to groups which were t work-related. Due to the lockdowns and shelter-at-home situations, there were suddenly lot of CFPs for online conferences. I spoke at seven online conferences, presented to two oups, participated in a panel, and led one workshop. I never imagined that I would meet my mple goal. A lot of the topics I presented were close to my heart: purple teaming ombination of blue team and red team activities), mental health and use of OSINT (Open-ource Intelligence) for good. I also got more involved with the different online infosec mmunities by volunteering at events and by mentoring other people. A lot of times, I don't enly talk about the things I've done to help others due to privacy needs.

ove working in the field of infosec and I wish that we had more diversity in this industry. ut it is discouraging when there is a lot of gatekeeping that hinders young graduates and reer shifters from getting into this field. For those of us working in this field, we need to ork with the business decision makers to create opportunities for meaningful internship periences and entry-level positions. In order to support women who typically bear the rden of unpaid emotional labor, we need to have flexibility in the workplace. We all come om different backgrounds and we don't always have the same paths to infosec. Thus, we so need to provide mentorship opportunities.

m at the point when I feel that everything that happened before is a preparation for the next allenge in my life. My past experiences have shown me that kindness has a boomerang fect; that tenacity in the face of adversity will eventually lead to attainment of my goals; at the hunger for knowledge must be balanced with sharing my expertise with those who ed it, and that the infant that shouldn't have survived can grow and thrive in another untry.

Chapter 10

Name: **Alexandria Horne**
Job Title: **Faculty, Web Design and Development**
Company: **Clark State College**
Location: **Cincinnati, Ohio, USA**

Although I am now an accomplished software engineer, the thought of pursuing programming or cybersecurity as a career never crossed my mind until my mid-20s. In fact, I took a C++ elective in college and hated it!

Growing up, I waffled between wanting to be a meteorologist, veterinarian, or marine biologist. At one point I even convinced myself I could do all three!

My upbringing was nothing unusual: I grew up in Troy, Ohio, a northern suburb of Dayton. My family was more or less the typical middle-class American household. My mother worked as a nurse; my father worked in HVAC for several years before purchasing a plot of land and becoming a farmer. I have two older brothers with whom I have been battling since before I could walk. Growing up, I found myself doing whatever my father and brothers were doing. My father coached my brother's little league baseball team and I quickly found myself the only girl on the team. Football, basketball, paintball, working on cars, racing go-karts and motorcycles were not unusual on any given weekend.

My mother is from a close-knit family of ten children, seven of them women. All my aunts have powerful personalities and never had a problem making themselves heard. With this influence in my childhood, it never occurred to me that "science was not for women." Many weekends were spent with cousins, aunts and uncles boating, fishing, and camping in northern Ohio.

As a child, I would try to spend every waking moment outside. I was (and still am) fascinated by everything in the world around me: plants, animals, clouds, rocks, soil, etc. Some of my favorite childhood memories include catching fireflies (or "lightning bugs" as we call them in Ohio). I would torture my mother each summer by taking cicada exoskeletons off nearby trees, hooking them to my shirt and chasing her around (she is not a fan of bugs). She loves telling the story of how one day while holding me as an infant, she noticed a large spider on her shoulder (she swears it was the size of a tarantula, though my father remembers it being a "small house spider") she promptly "tossed" me across the room onto a nearby couch and ran around the house screaming until she could dislodge it.

It's hard to grow up in Dayton, the "Birthplace of Aviation," and not be fascinated with airplanes. Trips to the Dayton Air Show were an annual tradition. My father regularly took me to the nearby National Museum of the U.S. Air Force and Huffman Prairie Flying Field, where the Wright Brothers made around 150 flights in the early 1900s leading to the development of the Wright Flyer III. That fascination encouraged me to earn my pilot's license at age 18. Another aspect of living in the Dayton area is its unfortunate history of being ground-zero for major midwestern tornado outbreaks. Oddly enough, my father always seems to find himself in the middle of these outbreaks. Growing up, he would tell me stories of surviving the 1974 tornado which struck the nearby community of Xenia, Ohio, killing 35 people. This F-5 tornado, at the time, was one of the largest and most powerful tornadoes on record. For Xenia, disaster struck again on September 20, 2000 when a large F-4 tornado tore through the community. Yet another struck the town 14 years later. As if Mother Nature wasn't satisfied by her earlier attempts, in May of 2019, the Dayton region was struck by 15 tornadoes within a 24-hour period. Whether it was motivated by fear or fascination, I developed a life-long passion for studying weather and climate.

After high school, I enrolled in the earth and atmospheric science program at Purdue University. I had an amazing time there and my professors were extremely supportive. With a student population of around 40,000 students, I met people from all over the world and experienced a variety of different cultures which I will cherish for the rest of my life. I graduated with my bachelor's degree in 2008. This seemed to be poor timing as the country was enduring the "Great Recession" and jobs were hard to come by.

I soon found myself at Ohio State University doing graduate work in natural resources and soil science. It was here that I was first introduced to programming, particularly Python which was used heavily in our Geographic Information System (GIS) driven research. After 18 months of study, I realized I wasn't a huge fan of Ohio State's culture; there seemed to be more focus on athletics than academics. My particular department was poorly funded and led by a tenured professor who focused almost exclusively on his publication tally and cared little for students. In 2010, I transferred to the University of Cincinnati's geography graduate program. There I was able to build my programming skills, becoming proficient in GIS eventually leading to completion of my Master's in 2011.

Struggling to find a job post-graduation, I spent the following winter de-icing aircraft on third shift at the Cincinnati/Northern Kentucky International Airport. To say it was a "unique" experience would be an understatement. I once again found myself as the only female in the group. The "Cincinnati" Airport is actually located in Kentucky. My co-workers, for the most part, were friendly, good-hearted men who were never short of a good story and were by far the most interesting group of people I have ever worked with. Many of them carried around Mountain Dew bottles and used them as "spit cups" for their chewing tobacco, a common practice in Kentucky. One slow night, they convinced me to try some; I could understand the appeal but was definitely not a fan. The job required de-icing trucks to be ready and on the "ramp" any time icing conditions were expected. We would listen for de-icing requests via airport departure traffic radio. Once a de-icing request came, time was of the essence as aircraft were de-iced just minutes before their scheduled departure. It was not uncommon to spend an entire 12-hour shift on the ramp with no break. This led to some very interesting situations, especially when someone had to use the "facilities." I would often see my male co-workers jump out of their de-icing truck, pee on the tire, and hop right back in. I remember on my first day, as we left our meeting room and jumped in our trucks one of the managers motioned for me to roll down the window. I saw that he had a roll of toilet paper in his hand. He leaned in and said "so…uh…most nights we don't really have time for…you know…bathroom breaks." I could tell it was an awkward situation for him. I reached for the toilet paper and laughed, "I'll manage" I replied. Never would I have imagined myself hiding behind a de-icing truck with my pants around my ankles at a public airport, but there I was.

On one particular night when we were quite busy, a co-worker came running towards me, waving his arms. I rolled down the window and asked: "Is everything ok?" Without hesitation, my co-worker responded: "No! I have to take a shit; can I borrow your toilet paper roll?" Equipped with said roll of toilet paper, he then crouched under the fuselage of a bright yellow DHL Boeing 747 and "did his business." I guess that situation would have bothered most women, I found it somewhat entertaining. I guess I had my earlier experiences with my brothers to thank for that!

Winter came and went, and I was able to find a job working as a geospatial technician at an engineering and geospatial firm in Dayton, Ohio. There, I was able to refine my programming skills and pick up a few new languages. Though many languages were used, Python was essential and allowed us to automate the processing of our airborne and terrestrial LiDAR data. For the most part, I had a pleasant experience there. The work could be monotonous at times, but I had a great boss, great co-workers who were always willing to mentor, and made lifelong friendships. At the time, a co-worker was taking courses at nearby Clark State College and mentioned that the college needed an adjunct instructor for its remote sensing course. So, I signed up and had a great time teaching there.

A few years later, a colleague from graduate school reached out asking whether I would be interested in joining his team as they were looking for a senior programmer. A few months later, I was hired on as a senior computer programming analyst at the City of Cincinnati's GIS department known as the Cincinnati Area Geographic Information System (CAGIS). Here, I was thrown into just about every type of programming you could imagine. It was also where I got my first taste of gender discrimination and retaliation in the workplace. At that time, the city was run by a ruthless city manager and a corrupt city council. Fortunately, our GIS group was jointly run by the City of Cincinnati and Hamilton County (the county in which Cincinnati resides) so we were somewhat shielded from the wrath of the city manager. In fact, our team led the city's digital transformation and won several national awards while doing so. To say my boss was not a huge fan of women would be accurate but in general, he treated most of his staff poorly regardless of gender. During a staff meeting, one of my male co-workers had a panic attack so severe, they had to wheel him out of the office on a stretcher; he resigned two weeks later. After this incident, I approached our human resources department and the city's employment union with concerns about how our staff were treated. The union representative was brutally honest, saying the union was aware of the behavior but could not do anything about it since my boss had the support of both the city manager and city council.

Cincinnati is a place where racial tensions run deep. The city has a long history of "race riots" dating back to the 1700s. The 2001 Cincinnati riot was, at the time, one of the largest urban riots in the U.S. The riot was triggered by the fatal shooting of an unarmed African American teenager by Cincinnati police. History would repeat itself on July 19, 2015 when, just a few miles north of our office, an unarmed African American man was fatally shot by a white University of Cincinnati police officer during a traffic stop. In the days that followed, the Hamilton County prosecutor announced that he would be pursuing murder changes. The Fraternal Order of Police was outraged and insisted that the shooting was justified. The city was in chaos yet again. One could "feel" the tension when walking around the city. One morning, a supervisor stopped by my desk and said, "we are sending everyone home at noon today, the body cam footage from the shooting is going to be released and we do not know how the city is going to react." As expected, there were demonstrations around the city that evening.

A few months later, a co-worker and I were looking out from my manager's 10th floor office window down at the front entrance of the county courthouse which was just across the street. The verdict of the trial was to be announced that day. There were a few dozen people gathered on the courthouse stairs: a mix of media and demonstrators. I saw a sudden bustle of activity from the nearby media vehicles and saw reporters sprint towards the entrance of the courthouse. What I saw next broke my heart. I watched as the mother of the slain man stumbled out of the courthouse doors and collapsed to her knees; she was in unimaginable grief. Two family members rushed to her aid, helping her down the stairs to a nearby vehicle all while being swarmed by members of the media. It had not yet been publicly announced, but we knew immediately what the verdict was. I can remember walking past the courthouse on my way to the parking garage that evening after the crowds dispersed. I stopped for a moment to read one of the quotes engraved on the outside of the building: "Equal and Exact Justice to All Men of whatever state or persuasion, religious or political." A knot formed in the pit of my stomach. All I could do was shake my head and walk away. Closer to the parking garage, I was approached by a disheveled man whom I assumed was homeless (this was not an uncommon occurrence working in Cincinnati's downtown business district). The middle aged African American man walked up to me, pulled out a small knife and said aggressively "now it's our turn, how would you like it if I murdered your babies?" I stood there at a loss for words before finally responding "you know what man; I honestly wouldn't blame you." Just then a young African American man saw what was happening and ran across the street to my defense. The man yielding the knife spat at my feet and walked away. I shudder to think what would have happened if he had not interfered.

The fight for racial equality in Cincinnati continues to this day…

A few years later, a local news story about a local teen who died in a tragic accident caught the city's attention. The 16-year-old named Kyle, somehow became pinned by a third-row seat in the back of his van. Kyle called 911 as he was suffocating and begged for help. Officers were dispatched but could not locate the boy. Kyle called 911 once again begging for help. He also left a heartbreaking message: "I probably don't have much time left, so tell my mom that I love her if I die." Again, a sheriff's deputy went to the scene, but didn't report seeing anything wrong. Several hours later, Kyle's father discovered his son trapped and unresponsive between the third-row bench seat and the van's back door. First responders were unable to revive him.

An investigation revealed that 911 dispatchers were unable to get proper information to officers on the scene because the 911 center's computer-aided dispatch system was "acting up." My co-workers and I were devastated. Had we known about the issues with their system, we could have integrated our GIS technology to create what's known as a "smart 911" system. This would have enabled police to find Kyle by allowing dispatchers to relay the approximate position of his cell phone. It was later revealed that Cincinnati's 911 service had been "acting up" for years. Several internal complaints were filed over those years, but nothing was done. This incident forced the city to evaluate its system and address the poor management and lack of staffing throughout the city.

These failures would not have been made public if it weren't for an amazingly brave city employee who we'll call "Betty." Betty was a programmer for the city's 911 center. She penned a scathing memo revealing that dysfunction fostered by poor management at the city's 911 center "poses a threat to members of the public." Her memo was made public by a local news station. Betty also exposed the "pattern and practice of unlawful and unconstitutional retaliation and intimidation of the city employees." She filed a retaliation lawsuit against the city manager; one of six city employees to do so. Though Betty chose to leave the city, her actions prompted the city council to force the corrupt city manager out of his position in 2018. Little did I know that only a few years later, I would find myself following in Betty's footsteps by challenging one of the most corrupt and dangerous companies in the world….

Disgusted by these events, I resigned from my position a few weeks later. In my exit memo, which I sent to the City's employment union, human resources, and city council, I described how poorly our staff were treated and detailed the dysfunction and lack of accountability that occurred in our department as well. I did not have another position lined up at the time but could no longer, in good conscience, continue working there.

few months later I began my first "official" cybersecurity role at GE Aviation as a software engineer. I was part of a team of developers tasked with protecting the company's intellectual property (IP) through digital loss prevention (DLP) and insider threat detection.

When I began at GE, I was thrilled. Once again, I was the only woman on the team, but I had grown used to that. My colleagues seemed great, my boss seemed supportive and it seemed the company was full of opportunities for ambitious developers. Unfortunately, first impressions can be deceiving. Time would reveal a culture dominated by fear and intimidation. Management had little interest in improving products or building strong teams. Instead, management focused on their next career move while their teams and products decayed.

Preventing IP theft is a difficult task in the best of circumstances as it requires analyzing user characteristics, monitoring devices, predicting behaviors, etc. Without supportive and knowledgeable leadership, our team had no chance of success. Over the year that followed, I discovered that the company had zero interest in complying with cybersecurity standards mandated by many of their federal contracts. Even worse, employees who raised concerns about these compliance failures were promptly retaliated against. Unfortunately, I was one of those employees.

The number of cybersecurity vulnerabilities present at GE was astounding. As if this wasn't enough, I soon learned that fraud, retaliation, and systemic discrimination were not only common, but encouraged at nearly every level of management. Gatekeeping, "mansplaining", refusing to let women speak, sexual harassment, and having co-workers sabotage each other's work was commonplace. Minorities and LGBTQ individuals were treated just as poorly as women at the company. After raising concerns and realizing that the company had zero interest in achieving compliance or improving its culture, I asked to be transferred to a different working group. The following day, I was escorted out the building. In the following year I reached out to countless other GE employees (past and present), documented hundreds of accounts of abuse, filed complaints with several federal agencies and worked with legal consultants to determine the best course of action to end the abuse. Then, we took action.

I posted on social media outlining the hostile work culture faced by female and minority employees of GE. I detailed accounts of how the company's human resources department refused to investigate or discipline dozens of male managers, many of whom had multiple complaints filed against them. In addition, I explained how the company uses its internal "integrity" complaint system, forced arbitration, attorney intimidation and unethical non-disparagement clauses to cover-up its illegal treatment of employees. My posts were shared widely throughout the company and prompted external investigations that would eventually confirm these accounts of abuse. The fallout ultimately forced GE Aviation CEO David Joyce to resign and set in motion what could potentially become a much-needed cultural reset at GE. My experience at GE made me realize that I could be an influential force for women in STEM. I continue to work with my former colleagues to expose the full range of abuses at GE and work towards better legislation and workplace protections for women.

"They" say you learn more from a bad boss than from a good one. Despite the hell I went through at GE, I did learn a number of very valuable lessons; one being that large companies like GE are never going to enforce cybersecurity standards fully. Taking legal action may help, but it's no silver bullet. I've concluded that the best option to combat this is to train developers to incorporate cybersecurity in every step of the software development life cycle, from planning, all the way through production and maintenance. As the saying goes: "the best defense is a good offense." Teaching developers how to create secure code from the start will go a long way in decreasing cybersecurity vulnerabilities like those seen at GE.

Shortly after being forced out of GE, Clark State College, where I had been an adjunct instructor several years prior, gained approval to create a web design and development baccalaureate program. The college needed a faculty member to create and coordinate this program. A few weeks later I was hired. I now have the opportunity to develop a program that emphasizes secure development as a coding standard. My teaching and advising responsibilities also allow me to mentor students, encourage more women to enter STEM fields and coach them through many of the hurdles they will likely face once entering the workforce. I also get to work closely with the faculty at Clark State's Center for Cyber Defense Education which is part of their cybersecurity and Information assurance degree program.

So, here I am. I'm not a meteorologist, veterinarian, or marine biologist, but I have found a way to earn a living while pursuing my passions. If it weren't for my experience watching "Betty" stand up and tell her story, I don't know if I would have had the courage to do the same.

The best advice I can give women entering the cybersecurity (or any STEM) field is to **know your rights** and **know your worth**.

Find your voice and don't be afraid to make it heard!

Maya Angelou said it best:

"Each time a woman stands up for herself, she stands up for all women."

Chapter 11

Name: **Shipra Aggarwal**

Job Title: **Cyber Security Expert**

Company Name: **SAP Labs India**

Location: **Bangalore, India**

My cyber security journey is quite unique, and it was unlike many of you, not by choice but by chance. Right now, I am very grateful for what I have achieved, and am honoured to have met outstanding colleagues all over the world. With this, I am extremely delighted to share my roller coaster journey from being a topper in school and an extremely introverted person, to becoming a real security expert, speaker in numerous external events and constantly working on myself to claim my place in the industry. I really hope to inspire each of you!

The beginning

I have my roots in Hyderabad (the city where Microsoft's CEO Satya Nadella spent his early years) one of the big cities in India, known for nurturing engineers and doctors. Every high school student there is preparing to become either an engineer or doctor and if you end up taking any other profession, you are not successful in life. With my father himself being a Scientist with DRDO – an agency under the Ministry of Defence of the Government of India, it is not so difficult to imagine what I would be doing when I grew up.

Doing fairly good as a school kid, I was always one among the toppers but not very outspoken. I studied in a government school with very humble upbringings. With my interest in Maths and Science, and following the trend of becoming an engineer, I took to preparing for the engineering entrance exams in my high school devoting 100% to it. It was a very rigorous continuous preparation of study 12-14 hours every day without any break for two years.

In 2002 my hard work paid off and I managed to get into the top engineering college of the state – Osmania University College of Engineering, by securing 200 odd rank among 1 Lakh plus students who sat the exam. Electronics and Communication was the first choice among students back then which I managed to get into. I was over the moon and felt like my life was set. However, a few weeks into the college, I soon found myself struggling to survive with the toppers all around the state. At this point like many other students, I didn't have much clarity in what my career or job would look like. I was invested in learning my subjects and getting a decent score.

My first job

With all the ups and downs I did finally get a bachelor's degree in 2006 and with high expectations of entering the corporate sector and motivation to change the world, I got placed in a reputed software giant. There were intellectual students from all over the country entering the firm in batches and going through all the basic soft skills and technical trainings. However, there was no plan to absorb us into projects; we soon realised computer science graduates were given a higher priority while many of us were kept waiting months to get a decent project. All our dreams started shattering in the first year and we started looking for better opportunities elsewhere. After almost one year and with the job market not very strong, I was minded to accept anything that came my way. It was then I was made through a position in manual testing with SAP Labs India in mid-2007. Only after joining I came to know it was for application security and felt hopeful as security was gaining prominence at that time.

As you see I had no background in cyber security education, all the knowledge I gained was directly while doing my job. Slowly I started learning and gaining experience in OWASP top 10, penetration testing or ethical hacking, DAST tools, web application security, vulnerability assessment and so on. However, I was still not a very outgoing person and liked to be by myself. I had an extreme fear of public speaking and found it very difficult to adjust to the corporate culture which has its foundation in presenting oneself, communicating, showcasing your achievements, and networking. Some colleagues found it easy to put me down thinking that I wouldn't speak up. Soon I realised that I need to get confidence in myself in order to reflect my potential in my performance. Even if I started to become more withdrawn, I was still not able to accept that being such an intelligent student all my life, compared to my peers, I was still not "feeling enough". In my mind I never gave up and I always believed in myself and, mostly important, I totally realised that security was my journey.

Within 3 years, I pushed myself to speak on security topics to around 100 participants at customer and partner events. My anxiety was undoubtedly through the roof, but that was one of my first experiences of facing my biggest fear. I felt great and learnt one of life's big lessons - *the best way to gain confidence is to act*. I didn't become a natural people person or an extrovert overnight but got the courage to take up such opportunities and get accepted in the corporate culture. In another couple of years, when giving a dry run for a talk in one such event I was told it was one of the best talks they had heard, I couldn't believe my ears and that surely boosted my confidence in speaking.

"If you want to improve your self-worth, stop giving other people the calculator."

- *Tim Fargo*

After reading multiple books and listening to various podcasts and courses on public speaking and practising through the years, I would like to highly emphasize that- *public speaking is not a talent that you are born with, it's a skill that anyone can develop with practice*. Over time I have realized how true that is and only wish someone had told me that in the early stages of my career.

was getting good hands-on exposure to numerous SAP solutions while evaluating their compliance to SAP product standard security and developed a strong security-focused mindset by then, which helped me in my later roles.

Moving on to Security Response

In 2012, I felt the need to look for other opportunities. The cyber security world was still quite small and did not have so many diverse roles back then as we have now. In fact, there were a mere handful of security positions at that time in Bangalore. Cloud was still in a very nascent stage and infrastructure security also had very limited scope.

SAP Labs is a wonderful organization that cares for its employees and does every bit to make them happy and content with their life even beyond work. It has some of the best employee policies and culture that anyone can dream of in the corporate world. No wonder it is rated as one of the best places to work both in India and globally. Thus, I was seriously hunting for options within the company as there was no reason I felt I should look elsewhere.

Incidentally, there was a new team being set up for Product Security Response in Bangalore; still feel grateful being able to join it. Here my role revolved around dealing with external security reports on security vulnerabilities in SAP solutions and communicating with researchers and customers. With such knowledge and with my communication improving over time, I was excelling in my job and began taking up newer challenges. For the first time was getting the recognition I deserved, and which encouraged me to push myself through hurdles. I was soon leading monthly Security Patch Days for SAP, giving trainings, organizing team workshops and the like. This role gave me exposure to the world of the hacking community, bounty hunters, their mindset, skills, and tools they use to find vulnerabilities and gain media and public attention. The role was also very intense on communication skills, as I needed to balance the tightrope between developers and external researchers. Very frequently the team had to deal with instances where the engineering team refused to accept it as a valid submission and the researcher threatened to go public. Any slight slip in handling a report could result in a zero-day disclosure for SAP, which translates as putting thousands of SAP customers and SAP's brand at risk; hence requiring deeper technical understanding of the vulnerability to take the right stand.

This was also the phase when I embraced motherhood and went on maternity break. After six months I had to return, initially working from home and then full time by mid-2014. As any working mother, I had my share of challenges in balancing house and work simultaneously. Support from home and my team did make things easier to resume work. I have always seen my mom managing all household chores and raising kids almost all by herself; that gives me the courage and natural ability to handle things efficiently.

While I was regaining my space in the team, I soon found colleagues who had been a few years behind me were now moving ahead and taking up responsibilities that I had managed previously. Although I was prepared for a setback, it still took time for the reality to sink in. I came back stronger and my graph didn't go down. In fact, I was at the peak of my performance a few years into my working mom role. Motherhood shaped me to be a better professional, as it made me approach work with more purpose, to enhance my networking and people skills and to push me to be more efficient in every aspect. Empathy, humility, diligence, reliability, time management, high quality work are some qualities that come naturally to women and even more to mothers. It's only a matter of understanding and leveraging one's strengths and making the most of the given situations rather than seeing motherhood as a career hurdle. Of course, one cannot be present at every networking event, after office parties or take up ad-hoc travel requests at least for a few years. But if you are lucky enough like me to work for a company that supports a healthy work culture and not in a travel intensive job, it should not be very difficult to balance matters. It is always better to stay away from organizations that incentivize employees for showing up late for no reason.

Although it is sometimes impossible not to think about home while at work and vice versa, my sincere advice is to try and give 100% attention to both while at the office and at home. Worrying too much and becoming stressful over small things doesn't help. Be comfortable when things do not go as perfectly as you would wish. Soon you will realise the important things in your life that you should care about and those you can't; let go as you can't have it all. You can easily manage kids, home, and work if you want to, provided you have that push within yourself. Nothing in life comes free, right? At the end of the day, if I get an opportunity to make decisions, stand on my feet and feel liberated then I am content. I would also like to quote Facebook COO Sheryl Sandberg's advice to – "*make your partner a real partner*" - dividing the chores wisely does help a lot. It may not be possible for everyone, but I see this as a major factor for a woman to succeed.

The shifting cyber security paradigm

Many open-source vulnerabilities made it to media in 2014 like Heartbleed, Shellshock, Poodle and zero-day disclosures in Internet Explorer, Adobe etc, cyber security and Product Security Response gaining utmost significance in the industry. Indeed, this was the decade when cyber security went mainstream; the shift in mindset from defensive to preventive was clearly being seen.

Since we were releasing security patches to customers, we learnt how they consumed them. Another key accomplishment for me during this time was driving Customer Engagement Initiatives for the response team with some of the top customers. During 2015 and 2016, I was responsible for hosting customer workshops at their locations, and continuously engaging with them to improve their patching experience holistically, eventually helping them secure their landscapes. With this initiative, we were able to significantly improve the

ality of security patches shipped by SAP over time and build strong relationships with our
stomers.

ing top performer year after year, in 2015 I was one of a few selected women employees to
dergo the prestigious LEAP (Leadership Excellence Acceleration Program), a 12-month
ng extensive program to groom us on various leadership aspects in networking and
anding, storytelling and communication, emotional intelligence, and developing political
vvy. This was one of the turning points in my career in terms of networking with highly
otivated women colleagues across organizations and getting a diverse view of their roles,
allenges, leadership styles. It undoubtedly helped me grow professionally in various
adership qualities. I started thinking more about my career and sought coaching sessions
d professional guidance on progressing my career. During this time, I also certified myself
a Project Management Professional in 2017, as I felt these skills would be relevant in
ery domain.

early 2018, I went on maternity leave while expecting my second child. This time I was
uch better prepared to deal with the situation, becoming more confident in returning
noothly to my career. Although it was sometimes very stressful and demanding to take care
the needs of everyone in the family, I was hopeful things would get better. Time flew and I
as back at work by mid-2018, settling down to new responsibilities such as managing Bug
ounty programs and leading CVE submissions for SAP, along with my core tasks in dealing
ith external vulnerability reports.

he evolving era of hyperscalers

multaneously, the digital landscape was changing drastically with cloud technologies
ining momentum and SAP accelerating its cloud strategy to stay ahead in the game. There
ere too many changes happening too quickly in terms of SAP's organizational structure and
iorities that also impacted the way we work, which nobody has been used to. Before it had
ly been a private cloud; then in 2015-16 hybrid cloud models started emerging. Slowly we
arted moving to the public cloud and then into the multi-cloud era. Big banks were moving
Azure platform, GCP, and AWS. We started seeing major shifts in the cyber landscape.
curity which had once been seen as a concern to move to cloud now started becoming an
abler; large enterprises began moving there to run their businesses. The use of public cloud
frastructure has grown dramatically over the past couple of years, with resources deployed
ughly doubling annually. The scale is truly remarkable - SAP now runs over 7.5 million
oud resources across 8,000+ active cloud accounts, across AWS, Azure and GCP, and
libaba Cloud and is projected to double in size each year for the near future.

curity in hyperscalers was suddenly gaining importance and with the EU adopting the
eneral Data Protection Law (GDPR) in 2016, Data Protection and Privacy became even
ore relevant. Many new roles started emerging in cyber space such as for example Red
eam, Blue Team and now Purple Team, Incident Response Analyst, SOC Analyst, Threat
telligence, Digital Forensics, Data Privacy officer, Risk Management, Security Auditor,
d Cloud Security Administrator. Artificial Intelligence is now being used to defend against
ber-attacks. Consequently, the demand for security professionals started rising

exponentially. Within a few years, the workforce of security professionals was and is multiplying throughout the technology industry. I was quite overwhelmed by these evolving dynamics and felt the strong need to upskill myself in cloud security topics and the latest technology trends. I started reading and attending webinars more often. Meanwhile I also gained certification in AZ-900 Microsoft Azure Fundamentals in order to become acquainted with the fundamentals of cloud infrastructure.

Then the pandemic hit us all; overnight our lives turned upside down. My work life balance took on a whole new meaning with schools and daycares shut, no household help and fully trapped inside the house. It took me a couple of months to get back on track taking short breaks from work and accepting the situation. It was not easy for anyone, but I always believe in William Shakespeare's words – "*Adversity brings out the best in man*". One has to rise to the occasion, be on guard, put up the best fight to make one stronger, bolder, and wiser. I was ready to make the best of this new life and took it as an opportunity to cultivate new hobbies. I started listening to audiobooks on leadership and self-help, devoted every available time to upskilling and expanding my professional network. I began attending virtual conferences, a new reality that opened up a lot of free networking opportunities while staying at home. At this time, I joined – Women in CyberSecurity (WiCyS) India, where I met many amazing women in the industry. I began speaking at many internal and external forums and looking for opportunities to enhance my skill set in DevSecOps, cloud security. After a few attempts I took up this exciting cyber security expert role with SAP Customer Experience, where I am responsible for uplifting the application security posture of cloud solutions in the portfolio. I am learning many new things, gaining the experience I sought; I am currently also preparing for a couple of cloud security certifications.

"*Choose to become the best version of yourself and not a product of circumstances*".

Before concluding, I would like to share few important pieces of advice that have shaped me to be the professional I am today:

- **You learn most when swimming in uncomfortable water.**
  Don't be afraid to take up opportunities beyond your skill set. If you have the strong will to learn, believe me you will find ways through it. Don't be afraid to fail. Learn from your mistakes. This is one thing I have learnt and realised time and again through every stage of my career.

- **Face your biggest fears.**
  It will not be easy but believe me the joy and confidence you get after it cannot be measured. You will come out stronger and satisfied.

- **Be vocal to claim your achievements.**
  Don't expect others to acknowledge your hard work automatically. It's a highly competitive world and no one has time to analyse the quality of work unless they hear from others and most importantly you, of what you have achieved. Get comfortable advocating for yourself.

- **What got you here will not get you to the next level.**
  As clichéd as it may sound, the earlier you realise this the better it is for your career as you climb up your ladder. Your people and communication skills, ability to understand organizational strategy and politics, mentoring junior colleagues to grow, discipline and ethics in your work and other soft skills will complement your technical skills.

- **Make a list of your strengths and leverage them wisely.**
  As touched upon above, take time to understand your strengths in both technical and soft skills and see how you can make use of them to become even better at them. Focus on one habit or skill at a time to improve.

- **Never stop looking for new opportunities.**
  Always be curious to learn every day. Try new things! If they don't work, try something else. The world is changing at a pace faster than ever and even to stay at our current position, we need to keep ourselves updated with the latest technologies. Learn the basics of cloud technologies, DevSecOps, hyperscalers to start with. Cyber Security is not just about penetration testing. Today we have tons of roles to explore and climb up.

- **Make the most of your online presence and make your way in.**
  Find and join cyber security communities in your area. I found LinkedIn to be an excellent platform to connect with professionals in your industry from entry level to CEOs and learn from them every day. I became aware of so many opportunities, courses, webinars, security communities and most importantly my daily dose of inspiration to progress my way through.

- My mentor once said – **Failure only hurts till the time you don't learn from it.** It made me look for learnings in every mistake, learn from every interview that I didn't clear, every opportunity that I missed. Instead of feeling guilty, find out what you can do so you don't repeat the error.

These tips might sound very simple but implementing such small habits can be life changing in your career and even personal life. All things said, in this race don't forget to take care of your physical and mental wellbeing. If you lose your health while running to get ahead, all your efforts are futile. Developing a regular workout routine even for 20-30 minutes helps.

Always feel free to reach out to me. I am open to help and support in whatever way I can and always looking forward to connecting with like-minded professionals and expanding my network and learning and sharing with the community. There has never been a better time to consider a cyber security career.

"When you truly study top performers in any field, what sets them apart is not their physical skill; it is how they control their minds."

- Stan Beecham

Chapter 12

Name: Jothi Dugar

Job Title: Chief Information Security Officer, Wellness Director,

International Best-Selling Author, and Public Speaker

Company: National Institutes of Health, Center for Information Technology

Location: Virginia, US

YOUR VOICE IS YOUR SUPERPOWER

Finding My Voice

I stood there standing as tall as I could, but I felt myself shaking inside. I told him in the bravest voice I could muster in a workplace setting yet keeping my calm to get out of my office before I call security. He stepped forward towards me, and just in that instant, I knew inside my heart that I had a choice to make, either take this treatment as one of many encounters I had experienced before and let it go OR stand up for myself. I had let things go enough in my life. I have gone through enough pain allowing and enabling people to walk all over me and treat me like I was a "nobody". This time was different, *I* was different. I got behind my desk which stood between him and me, and I picked up the phone and started dialing the Security department of my organization. He started to back off.

"What the heck are you doing?" he yelled as he took a step backwards. "You women just want to get us good men in trouble, don't you?" he screamed.

"I am calling Security because I asked you to leave my office and you are still here and I feel threatened." I answered as calmly as I could.

"Whatever! You need to just go back where you came from you little piece of sh***! I don't know why they ever let you out from your country." he roared as he started to walk back towards the door.

"Please leave right now." I said calmly but sternly as I walked towards him feeling as big as I could get myself to be.

I shut the door and crumbled to the floor crying. My heart was pounding a thousand beats a second and I couldn't breathe. I had a meeting in a few minutes, but I didn't care. I just let it all come pouring out. I did it. I stood up for myself and I made him go away. But I knew I had to do more than just that. I could not just let him go around treating people like that, especially women.

I called my boss and our Ethics manager and reported all the facts to them of what had just transpired. I told them how I tried my best to keep myself as calm as possible and did not engage in his atrocious behavior. I told them how I felt threatened and scared. I did not hold back. I knew I was worth it. I was worth protecting, I was worth having a voice and deserved to work in a safe and friendly environment.

My boss and my Ethics manager were appalled by the man's actions and immediately came over to assure me I had their full support and immediately reported the incident to our Civil department.

Just as they left, my next-door colleague came over and told me he had heard the whole thing and applauded me for my actions and how I dealt with this person.

"He's done this many times before to both men and women, and you are the first person to put a stop to his behavior." he said as he thanked me. I felt an immense weight in my heart just release. "Wow, little me put a stop to this big man?" I wondered.

I realized in that moment, that it was not about my physical strength, it was my character and mental strength that got me through this and break free from the cycle I had been in all these years. I had assumed that harassment and having to prove myself every day just for being a young, minority female wouldn't happen in senior leadership positions. Well, I guess I thought wrong.

Here I was, a Chief Information Security Officer (CISO) in a major prestigious, high visibility organization, with a dream office that most people only dream of, and an amazing environment to work in. I had made it big, throughout all the challenges and roadblocks that I passed through. No one is going to give me a hard time here now, I mistakenly thought.

And, yet here I was, having to fend off another guy that had an ego the size of the room who thought he could corner me into surrendering to his agenda just by physically and verbally threatening me.

But this time was different. I had found my voice, and I knew I deserved one. I had to use it for the good, not just my good but for everyone's good.

I found out a couple weeks later after going through the Civil process in my organization that he had been transferred to another department far away from my work unit and was counseled.

"Thank you, God." I prayed as I felt relief and strength at the same time.

The Masculine Mask

As I sat at the dinner table that night, I remembered all the times I thought I had to put on a masculine mask and a tough attitude just to get my next job. I had always been in male dominated fields ever since high school.

hile all other kids were busy playing with their friends and getting jobs as babysitters or eguards in neighborhood swimming pools in high school, I had been selected for a Merit holarship and military internship program. After four years in high school, I was working r the U.S. military in Walter Reed Army Institute of Research (WRAIR) as they called it at e time, learning a variety of subjects such as Biotechnology, Entomology, Immunology, d believe it or not, even Information Technology. I was one of the first people, let alone a mmer intern that had access to a computer and wrote a whole thesis paper on the Internet d the various search engines that existed at the time.

was an amazing experience working for the U.S. military starting from high school itself, d I continued working for them through my college years as well. I tried to vary my periences each year so that I wasn't set on learning just one field.

ad always thought growing up that I wanted to be a doctor, maybe a heart surgeon I gured. I even got into Penn State seven year pre-med/med program and had enough AP edits that put me almost in the second year of college as a Freshman in many of the medical urses.

owever, one day, a doctor walked into my Biology class as a guest and asked each of us hy we wanted to be a doctor. He talked about the years of hard work and dedication it ould take, and the kind of life we would have afterwards especially if we wanted to be rgeons.

hen it was my turn, I told him I just wanted to help people and I thought a doctor was the st field to be in to do that. He looked at me and laughed.

oung lady, there are a gazillion other fields and other ways you can help people. You don't ve to go through all this if that is your primary passion." he explained.

m still thankful till this day I had that awakening call. I realized that indeed, there were a zillion other ways and fields I could enter to help people, and in hindsight, I am so thankful did not become a western medical doctor (you'll see why later).

, after much consideration and searching for the best field, my parents convinced me to rsue Electrical Engineering with an emphasis on Networks and Computer Science. I had ready been exposed to Cryptography and Security through my internships with the epartment of Defense, however there were no Cyber security programs back then.

was definitely challenging but I persevered and graduated in three years from the niversity of Maryland as one of the youngest graduates and one of handful of females. In ct, I think I was one of two Indian American girls in my entire class. Ironically, the other dian American girl was also named Jyothi!

ulture, Communications, and cyber

graduated in possibly the best year, 2000, before the dot coms burst forth and companies d plenty of money to splurge. I joined Cap Gemini Ernst & Young and traveled the world exciting projects and had the amazing opportunity to experience different cultures and fferent people, languages, food, and ethnicities. It was truly the best time of my life!

really think experiencing other cultures, people, and figuring out how to speak different nguages and communicate was pivotal for my cyber leadership career. It really taught me be respectful towards everyone, and never judge others as I learned that what is considered tally acceptable in one culture is a big faux pas in another! I learned that even when two people did not speak the same language, they could still "connect" when both were interested in communicating with each other, and showed curiosity, compassion, and empathy towards one another. Boy have these come into play almost daily being a CISO even today!

Ageism

After five years traveling for work learning on the job and gaining valuable experience in various technical fields, I decided I wanted to go back to the Intelligence and Defense community and took on multiple roles with the Department of Defense as a contractor. I liked the DoD, but once again I was one of few females and really getting tired having to prove myself even after I got the job or the role. Not only was I a woman in what was just assumed to be a "male" role, but my "ageism" didn't actually help me either! When most people worried about looking older than they were or getting wrinkles, my biggest challenge was looking like I was twelve being a minority female lead in a male dominated environment that was not receptive to women to begin with.

Everywhere I worked, when I walked in the room, people mistook me to be the secretary or the assistant to someone in a higher position, or an intern, even after I was a decade past graduation. I still remember one of my jobs I took was being a military trainer where I had to travel to all the military bases around the U.S. training the military on the Defense Travel System, the latest and greatest system out there at the time.

I walked into the classroom along with my co-trainer, an older gentleman, and the whole class gave us a look of adoration. Adoration mind you, NOT *admiration*. Everyone was saying how cute "this" was, and I felt baffled. Within a few minutes as I began teaching the class, I felt an absurd silence and a look of astonishment in the faces of these military men with some of them being five-star generals or colonels. I had to stop the class and literally ask what was going on.

"Ok folks spill the beans. What's the elephant in the room? I can sense it!" I asked the class.

"Well ma'am, at first we all thought it was so cute that Don had brought his daughter to the class, until we realized you were not his daughter, but his co-trainer!" one of the students, a three-star general exclaimed. Well, as you can probably sense by now, this was not the first time or the last!

Starting in cyber

My cyber career started when my manager at the time (who is now one of my best friends and cheerleaders) told me he thought I should check out the cyber security field, it looked an interesting, and fairly new field he felt I had the skills and ability to learn. I looked into it and did a lot of research.

I didn't really know what it was all about as such, and whoever I saw in the field at the time (unfortunately, even now) looked the same...older "white" men.

As I had dealt with male dominated fields before I hesitated to get into yet another where everyone looked the same, except me.

However, my boss convinced me to take a couple training courses and try it out. My first course was the Ethical Hacking with which I immediately fell in love. I took on projects that were Cyber oriented and learnt a lot on the job. I volunteered for existing security teams in addition to my existing role at the time just to get additional experience in the field.

I thought I would stick to it for a couple years then branch off into other things, but here I am, fifteen years later, still in cyber!

I liked being in the technical cyber fields for a while, but I was soon being put into more leadership roles by my managers; eventually I realized I am a good manager, and a good leader. I was not only good, but I loved it. I loved seeing people grow and I loved being a leader who people naturally liked to follow and admired. All my travel experience and navigating my way through male dominated fields and experiences my whole life was helping me navigate being a cyber leader.

After almost a decade being a Defense Contractor, I decided to switch to the other side and join the Federal Government. I gained my cyber experience being an Information Systems Security Officer (ISSO) for several years with the Defense Information Systems Agency (DISA), Internal Revenue Service (IRS), and finally landed at the National Institutes of Health (NIH) where I have been the last ten years.

Being Grateful for Challenging People

When I first landed at the NIH, I felt so excited and honored to begin my new journey at the world's largest biomedical research organization which developed cures for illnesses and diseases where none existed. I had my first baby right before I joined, and as a new mom and a new manager in a new job, it was very challenging really to enjoy the moment. And then, there came the group of four men I had to manage as my direct reports.

Wow, what a rough four years! Now, when I look back at those years and the men I had to deal with, I am actually thankful for them. They made me who I am today; it didn't kill me but made me stronger! The four men, especially two of them who were leads, had applied for my job which both were expecting to get. So, when neither got it and they selected me, a young, minority female, a new manager and new to the NIH, things did not go well.

For four years, those two men continued to harass me, put me down, disrespect my authority as their manager, and did whatever they could to make my life miserable. In fact, when I got pregnant with my second baby three years in, they tag-teamed together to try and make my life so miserable that I would not want to come back after my maternity leave.

Trust me, I pondered the thought day and night in the middle of nursing a newborn baby and contemplating my career and path. I wondered if I should just quit and stay at home with my kids, or maybe find another job.

But I couldn't let these two immature, and childish men push me down. I had gone through enough traumas, roadblocks, and challenges in my life to know that I would never quit. I was not a quitter and would use the opportunity to bounce back being stronger and more resilient than ever before. I had to, not just for me, but for the organization, and the value I knew I added there. No one could take away my dignity or my value; I knew I had to go back.

As soon as I went back, one of them left for another job (Thank God!) and the other totally surprised me. He changed a whole 180 degrees for the better! I really could not believe it. He was suddenly kind and considerate. He was respectful in his tone, and words, and in fact he even had a sense of protection over me from some other bad characters in my environment. I did not know what had happened, but I remember asking him on his last day in the office a couple years later when he decided to get a promotion elsewhere what had made him change so drastically.

"Jothi, I really thought you would not come back after we gave you such a hard time. But, when you did, AND you continued to be professional and cordial with us, I really felt like you are a true leader, and one who I *needed* to respect. In fact, I want to apologize for all my behavior towards you. I now realize that it was my own insecurities that made me want to challenge you, not yours." he proclaimed.

That was one of the most profound moments of my life, and I still reflect on it every time I encounter a challenging situation at home or at work. Everything happens for a reason, and almost always by my showing up with all the strength and resilience that I have within me, not only makes me a better person, but also the person I am encountering!

What Does Cyber, Wellness, and Dance Have in Common?

My big break and really a changing point in my life came at the birth of my third baby. What was supposed to be the best days of my life having a newborn and two other amazing kids turned out to be a life and death experience leaving me with six weeks to live.

I had gone with a new OB for my third, and one who turned out to be negligent and incompetent to say the least. She had completely botched my C-section (this was my third, so I had assumed I knew what to expect) leaving me with a hip-to-hip incision, six inches of scar tissue all around my belly, with abdominal muscle layers not patched back together, two hernias, and my abdominal muscles separated by six inches. I could not move any part of my body without excruciating pain let alone hold the baby myself for over a year.

The OB went missing in action for the first four months, and I had no answers why all of this was happening to me. Even after seeing numerous surgeons with my CT scan results, I was getting completely different opinions, but they all said one thing, that if I didn't get one or more (without any clear indication of whether all my complications would be fixed or my full body excruciating pain would heal), I had six weeks to live.

I had a choice to make and it was a tough one. I decided that I no longer want to put myself under the care of the Western Medical Healthcare system. I started seeking alternative, holistic, natural wellness modalities.

And, as they say, when the student seeks answers, the teacher shall arrive. So, it did for me. Believe it or not, within six weeks I had found an energy healing therapy called Reiki and Chinese Traditional Medicine which heals hernias. Within six weeks my hernias had healed about 80% and my pain had started reducing as well. That gave me a tremendous amount of hope and faith, so I searched for more natural modalities.

Crossroads

It was definitely not an easy battle, but I was able to heal myself completely over the following three years. However, I could not stop there as I am a soul who loves to share with others and give back. I started learning numerous natural and holistic modalities and therapies and began my own Holistic Wellness practice as well as learning coaching.

Now I was at a crossroads. I was a CISO at a large government organization and loved my job. However, I also loved being a Wellness coach and practitioner, as well as a Dance Director (as I had also founded a dance company). What do I do? Do I need to leave cyber security to pursue my passion and mission of serving others through holistic wellness?

After much trial and error, contemplation, thought, therapy, reflection, and ups and downs, I knew that everything I was doing and everything I had experienced in my life thus far, were working *for* me, and they were ALL part of me. I didn't have to leave one for the other, and in fact I couldn't.

So, I started to take everything I had learned to heal myself in really understanding the mind-body-energy connection and how important that was and started to see how I could apply those principles. I knew there had to be a way because I was searching for it! I also realized after doing an extensive amount of research that clinician/healthcare burnout (which I believe is what had caused my OB to botch my C-section as I never got a straight answer from her as to why she committed such an atrocity and I never tool legal action) and Cyber security professional burnout had much in common.

In fact, the reasons for burnout in both industries were so similar that I knew I was on to something. I looked around in my own organization, and everywhere I saw, there were people that were burned out, tired, overwhelmed, getting sick, leaving, and just unhappy. I knew I had to do something, and I was placed there for a reason.

Cyber Wellness

I started integrating all my wellness modalities together and developed quick and easy wellness techniques/hacks that can be done anywhere, anytime, and only took a few minutes to do. I knew that Technology and Cyber leaders such as myself did not have the time of day or the patience to follow through on natural modalities like yoga or meditation that took up a lot of time. In fact, even if they did, those techniques by themselves were simply not enough to bring to the reality of the moment when it came to the chaos of the workplace or home.

I also knew that being in a male dominated environment, a lot of the natural wellness techniques or programs out there were not attracting many males especially in a workplace environment. I knew what I had to do! As I developed quick and easy techniques that could be implemented throughout the day causing a cumulative positive effect on a person's mind-body-energy, I also started to create terminology that really resonated with the Technology/Cyber professionals such as "Authentic Operating System", or the "Control-Pause-Delete method".

I also decided to be proactive about my mission to merge Holistic Wellness with Cyber security and started the first Health & Wellness program in my organization. I did all the work initially in setting it up, gaining interest and participation, getting the word out, and even teaching the majority of workshops. My workshops and my wellness program really took off and gained so much interest, that other departments and institutes within my agency also began participating and really has helped employees learn natural and holistic ways to heal themselves and thrive in their workplace and their lives.

The Mind-Body-Energy Connection in Cyber

Now, not only did I see a need to merge Cyber and Wellness together in terms of enabling the workforce to take on an approach of "the whole person comes to work" mindset prioritizing their wellness, but I also discovered the "mind-body-energy" holistic approach in the Cyber security field itself!

The mind or mindset of the organization and how it views Cyber is crucial for the success of a CISO or Cyber leader. If the mindset of leaders is that Cyber is a mission blocker or it is optional or unwanted, the first thing we need to do is to start to shift that mindset. As I had learnt in my healing journey, everything starts with our mind when it comes to our Wellness, and it is no different in Cyber security.

Now, the body as I saw it were all the tools and technology that are deployed across an organization. Often, organizations take the Western Medical System approach of putting "band-aid" fixes to squash the symptoms, versus digging deeper layers and solving the root cause of a problem. We need to change that approach in Cyber, and really take the time and effort needed to discover what exactly caused the problem to begin with. How do we have so many vulnerabilities? Was it a resource constraint issue? Was it a training/knowledge gap issue? Are there processes/procedures missing or not being followed?

Once we identify the root cause(es), then we can determine a "cure" which may or may not be a tool. We don't need to throw unnecessary tools into the mix unless there truly was a need as most organizations tend to have an oversupply of tools and technologies where there is a significant overlap of functions between tools, the majority of which aren't being utilized efficiently.

Now, the "energy" in the Cyber field is what I see as the culture of an organization. We need to understand the strengths of the culture and map our Cyber approach to the cultural strengths and demonstrate how Cyber enables these strengths. For example, in a research type organization, the culture is to share data, science, and research freely and openly with multiple organizations. As Cyber leaders, we cannot mandate that sharing of data should not be allowed for security concerns. It is our job and our role to enable that cultural strength of free and open sharing of data to collaborate by determining how we can share securely and safely while minimizing the risks.

Merging Cyber & Wellness - My Mission

As I started speaking about my Holistic & Integrative Approach to Cyber Wellness and gave keynote talks on it to various Cyber events and organizations that included Wellness hacks in them, I really started gaining national and international attention. I was sought by numerous event organizers, companies, and organizations to give talks and to conduct Wellness workshops and programs for their organizations. I even wrote a chapter in a book (see more at www.jothidugar.com/books) that became an International Best Seller on Amazon!

As I started to find my voice and purpose in the world, it was not all rosy and glam. I found that sometimes, not everyone is happy for you, especially when you seem to be succeeding and on an ascending path. A lot of times, it could be your own supervisor (who may be another woman and finds you a threat), or it could even be a family member or spouse. It is a hard challenge to navigate through; trust me when I say that you are being given these challenges and these people in your lives for a reason.

Shining Your Light

you're going through a challenging phase right now as a woman, just know you are ready for it. You wouldn't have this challenge land in your life if you weren't, and guess what? your whole life plus the experiences, skills, and growth so far has prepared you for this challenge. Think of it as another level that you must pass to move up to the next: amazing opportunities are awaiting you!

Whatever challenge you go through, please remember you are NOT alone, ever. As women, we try to be superwomen and do everything on our own. We must help and support each other. Don't hesitate to reach out and ask for help, remember YOU are the only YOU in the universe, so prioritize your own well-being. It is ok to be selfish about your own happiness, wellness, and health. If you're not, who else will be?

My last tip I'll leave with all you amazing women is never give up on your dreams and goals; always shine your light on others. There's always someone out there in the dark waiting for YOU to shine your light on them. It is ok to be the first person to try something new or a different approach or have a unique angle on a topic. Fitting in and staying in your comfort zone may seem safe and easy, but no one has ever accomplished anything great taking the easy way. You ARE great, so Just Go for It!

Chapter 13

Name: Aarti Gadhia

Job Title: Enterprise Cybersecurity Sales Canada & APAC

Company: Bugcrowd

Location: Vancouver, Canada

Jambo, Namaste, Konichiwa, Bonjour, and Greetings!

Thank you, Lisa, for creating this opportunity to share our experiences. As many are aware, the technology sector is male dominated. Promoting gender diversity in our industry is important, but it is easier said than done. Unconscious bias, second generation gender bias and systemic barriers exist for underrepresented groups, including women.

My mission is to break down barriers and boundaries to achieve equality for underrepresented groups in STEM and leadership. I'm sharing this journey through my unique experiences and my hope is to inspire everyone, that no matter what you're faced with, stay authentic, speak up for equality and don't be afraid of the outcome!

Let's get started with my background. I was born and raised in Nairobi, Kenya and am the youngest of three, and the only daughter. Both my parents unfortunately couldn't complete their studies and had to quit school to help their family earn a living. They were determined to make sure we all completed college and they got to fulfill their dreams through us. Ever since the age of five, my dad would take me to his place of work on weekends. He was an entrepreneur, and he ran a small business selling Japanese car spare parts. At that time, I didn't even know that sales could be a full-time profession. By observing the discussions taking place on the sales floor, I gained experience in learning to listen and communicate to customers. On Fridays after school, my mom would take me to "sokoni" which is a Swahili word meaning market. My task was to carry the "kikapu" (a basket made from sisal). I watched my mom negotiate and bargain with local merchants and little did I know at that time I was picking up an important soft skill that I would be applying not only in the workplace but generally in life.

Growing up, I always wanted to work in the stock market. The schooling system chose your path based on your grades. The top students were placed in sciences, the middle in business class and the bottom were assigned to arts. I fell in the category of business and at that time, I questioned why my future would be decided based on a grading system. If you were in a business or arts stream, the path was to study accounting at a local college and if you were a woman and didn't pursue further studies, you'd be married off. I was determined to follow my dream and wanted to experience University life abroad.

In 1997, we didn't have internet in schools to do the research, and we were supposed to choose a University based on an advertising brochure! I chose University of Wales, Swansea as it offered the degree I wanted to pursue, which was Financial Economics....and I loved the pictures of the campus located by the beach. At my first week at University, I had my worst experience thus far in life. I was away from home, away from family and in unfamiliar territory. On top of that, I had a very strong Kenyan accent that made me feel different from others. Students would sometimes ask me questions like how I can speak English so fluently or whether our house was a hut in a forest. Just to pull their leg, I would joke at times that I had lions as pets in my backyard.

During my first weekend, my roommates were going to a nightclub, and I went along with them, so I didn't feel left out. This was my first time going to a night club where I didn't know anyone. My roommates were interested in drinking and partying and I clearly remember they were taking off one after another leaving me all alone – I knew they were running away from me as I was different, and I didn't fit in! I could have changed who I was to try and fit in, but I didn't. I was alone and frightened, in a foreign country and didn't know how to get back to the campus. Finally, I left the nightclub and saw a phone booth and called my parents. It was 1am (4am in Kenya), I had three pounds which barely gives you three minutes of talk time in a phone booth. The next day I was feeling very down and wanted to quit University. I had to make the biggest decision of my life, give up and go back to Kenya or become a survivor and learn to accept who I am.

With both my brothers' encouragement and the help of the International Student Officer (who was incidentally from Kenya), I moved out of that unfriendly dorm to a much better one and my university experience from then on improved drastically. We all face ups and downs, and sometimes you will feel out of place and don't fit in. You may be the only female on your team as you join this industry. My first advice is don't change who you are, and stay true to your personal values, find your inner strength, and connect to your goals, motivation, and purpose.

This then leads me to share my second piece of advice which is to take the time to develop and practise your soft skills. Soft skills are life skills such as teamwork, empathy, networking, problem solving, creativity. If you've seen my post on LinkedIn titled "Phulka Roti" I share how I learnt how to make the Indian flatbread called "roti" while growing up. Initially for me it would take me 30 mins to make 20 rotis whereas now it takes me 10 minutes less for me to make the same amount. The soft skills I've gained over time in making roti are time management, speed, and accuracy – which equates to cost savings. Completing 10 minutes faster means I am saving gas/electricity, and now I have 10 minutes added back to my day. Especially today, with everyone being remote and living in a hectic world, time management is crucial. Soft skills are difficult to teach as they come with practice, experience, and ongoing feedback.

During my time at University, I took on a leadership position for a not-for profit organization called The Skills Society and was involved in scheduling workshops delivered by graduate recruiters. Other activities I was involved with that developed my skills further were volunteering my time to look after autistic kids on Sundays and taking seniors out for social evenings on Mondays. I also had a part time job at the student's union where I was allowed to work for a maximum of 20 hours per week. As I wasn't a UK permanent resident, it was quite costly and complicated getting sponsored for a work visa. In order to get more work hours during school breaks, I had to be creative. During my first summer holiday, I applied to be a counsellor in New York at a campsite working with kids who had dyslexia. My second summer break, I applied for a 12-week, government sponsored internship program where you were given a project to complete for an external organization and are entered to compete against other students for the Most Enterprising Student award. When I received the award, I realized how my soft skills helped me excel in the workplace and I started believing more in myself.

Cyber security roles require more than technical skills. Unfortunately, due to unconscious bias, many job descriptions and hiring managers shortlist candidates based on technical requirements. This is one of the main reasons why there is a cyber security staff shortage! In October 2020, I ran a fireside chat and all 4 of us ladies happened to join the cybersecurity industry by accident. Our backgrounds were in diverse fields such as project management, engineering, accounting, and economics and look at us now as we're all working in this industry. I've also seen a female who transitioned from HR to join the SOC team. Many hiring managers would not shortlist candidates if they do not have a technical background. A female CISO saw her potential as she was good at problem-solving and understanding human behavior and offered her the opportunity. In order to solve the cybersecurity gap, the challenge isn't that we don't have enough cybersecurity professionals graduating, the challenge is that we are limiting ourselves to traditional recruitment methods.

After graduation, The Skills Society where I was volunteering offered me a full-time position at their head office. The job required me to organize national events – I had to get sponsorships from companies and slowly found I was creating a position for myself which was to sell membership packages. This led to my promotion into management where I headed the membership department.

In 2004, I was ready for the next chapter. My husband proposed and I packed up in UK, we got married in Kenya and settled down in Vancouver, Canada. As a new immigrant, it wasn't easy getting a job. Today, when I meet many new immigrants, I go out of my way to help them find a job by introducing them to my network. I remember I applied everywhere for sales and management positions but didn't land any interviews. I started networking and that led me to connect with a recruiter who was also an immigrant from UK. She informed me about an entry level position at an anti-virus company. At that time, I didn't care what position was offered or what industry it was in, I just needed a job in order to settle down fast.

Before that, the only exposure I had related to the cyber security industry was at University. I remember asking my lecturer for an extension on a project as my 3M floppy disk (remember those square disks?) got corrupted due to a virus. I'll share a little secret… despite having to rewrite my project (which I hadn't spent much time on) for once, the virus actually saved the day!

With so many new threats and tactics emerging each day, I know that by joining this industry, I am contributing to a greater vision to keep our digital world safe from cyber-attacks. I started off in sales development, moved into customer success, then to inside sales and now in field sales.

In most of my career in cyber security field sales, I have been either the only female or one of the few females on the team. I think there's two parts why this is: a lack of awareness about this profession and industry and the general assumptions made about a woman's ability to be a success at this role.

Focusing on the first part, I found that a lot of students didn't have knowledge about the role or industry. When I sat on a panel, I told a group of students about what I did and how I go about it. A lot of them assumed that if you work in cybersecurity, you were someone who sits behind a computer and does coding. I had to explain that working in this industry isn't purely engineering, and there are other opportunities to make a lot financially and grow your career. The cyber security industry is very diverse and has several different positions and roles. I hope more schools teach kids that there's more to cybersecurity than just the coding part.

As for the second part, in 2005, when I started off as a Sales Development Rep, I was the number one performer on the team. I remember at one point, my manager pulled me aside to inform me that my success was breaking the commission calculator and his budget! This was an indication for me to move into an Inside Sales position. I applied internally and a part of the interview process involved filling a "personality test". The belief was that men were more successful in this role because they were outgoing / extroverts, and they had the gift of the gab. Sales isn't about talking, rather it's about listening. I knew that curiosity and listening were important, and I stuck with it. I thought that my performance and proven success would get me that position but unfortunately, the results of my personality test put me in the category of an introvert and the hiring director didn't believe I'd be successful.

Thankfully, another Director gave me a shot. Through my performance I proved many leaders wrong. This led to getting rid of the personality test that was a barrier not only for me but also for women within that organization to get into cyber sales positions.

The reality is often women will not get recognition for a job well done and will be wrongfully blamed for failure. At our annual sales kick off conference, I didn't receive an award despite being the top performer in the organization. Many leaders knew this was wrong, but no one spoke up for me. I knew I had to fight this on my own and I raised several questions and received inconsistent answers from different leaders. As a result, the company decided to create a clear set of rules for the "Salesperson of the Year" award. This removed a bias within that organization so that women are equally recognized for their performance.

This explains my third advice: Don't let anyone tell you that you're not good enough. Focus your energy on your mission and you'll see the results of your efforts and prove them wrong! The world is changing and we're seeing women as top players in organizations. My success has brought a lot of visibility in terms of women being successful in this role. This helped women who didn't see field sales as an option now get inspired to move into the role.

Many leaders have provided me advice to network internally and outside of my department in order to progress in my career. Many times, I felt I had a disadvantage as I didn't attend office meetups after work. I soon learnt that networking doesn't need to be an afterhours thing or going to a bar. Networking can simply be a coffee meeting to get to know someone within your organization. With the pandemic today, travel and in-person meetings are not happening and the only way to network is virtual. A great way is to create a slack group with a fun element for example, a virtual health fitness group or a scavenger hunt.

We've all had a journey where we have faced a bias. I was faced with several obstacles in this industry to get into senior leadership positions. I was given all sorts of reasons over the years:

1- Your location is a barrier for your promotion.
2- You don't have experience in senior executive roles.
3- You need to network beyond the sales function.
4- You need to make the ask.
5- You need to be more vocal and visible.

I am sure at some point in your career, you will have heard of some of these reasons. Five years ago, I was browsing LinkedIn and began reconnecting with some of my colleagues. I noticed that many had progressed in their career and were in Senior Executive positions. I spoke to two individuals to find out what they did, and their advice was "Make the ask" – sounds simple right?

A major challenge I have had in my career is that I reported to 17 different managers at the five organizations I have worked for. Each time, at the moment I started to build some momentum, the manager would either move up or left for another organization or they didn't want to support my career progression. I knew I needed to find a steady mentor who would be there for help and support throughout my career. It sounded easy, as all I needed to do was to "Make the Ask" but I was afraid, because if I chose someone at an executive level, they would see my weaknesses and I felt it could possibly ruin my chances of career growth.

hen I did not get an internal promotion, I felt I had nothing to lose and I asked that ecutive if he would be willing to be my mentor and luckily, he agreed. A few months later, persevered again and found my next mentor outside the industry. This then leads to my urth tip and advice, which is the importance of finding the right mentor and sponsor and dicating some time every month towards your personal development. Last year, one of our ecutives asked me to be his mentor – a process called reverse mentoring as he was at a gher level within the organization than I was. We committed to meeting semi-monthly - hile I was mentoring him, he also became my sponsor. We got inspired to develop a entoring program that we felt would benefit the staff immensely, and we called it Mentor-atch. It was similar to a dating site where you sift through suitable options and find your atch.

he reason many individuals don't have a mentor today is either because they are fearful of king someone or that they don't make it a priority and time becomes an excuse. If you ked me 3 years ago whether I would be able to start up an organization or be a voice or ride motorbike, I would say "are you crazy?". I once followed advice from one of my sponsors how to create my own path for a career progression in leadership. Unfortunately, this sulted in a negative response from upper management and I was faced with icroaggression. It hurt and I couldn't sleep for two weeks. As I shared this to my sponsors d mentor, they started to see what women are faced with daily. I am happy to say that my entors reminded me of my mission and that encouraged me to speak up! My mentors have ided me successfully and here I am living beyond what I can achieve.

2018 when the organization was preparing for a Sales Kickoff event, I reached out to my ternal mentor to help me become a speaker at the conference. He introduced me to a few of e speakers he knew who were leading various sessions. Three times out of three, I was told anks but no thanks! My mentor started to see the challenges women faced and began to see ings through my lens.

decided to carve out my own opportunity and I reached out to the Chief People Officer and e of the members from the steering committee to discuss an opportunity. My idea was to ld a 45-minute fireside chat to highlight the importance of diversity in the workplace and t the spotlight on women within the organization. Both leaders wanted to support this itiative and pitched this to the rest of the committee. Despite it being too late to make anges to the agenda, they agreed to a grassroots approach and we were given a breakout om for 40 attendees over lunch break. I was thrilled – I didn't get what I wanted but at least wasn't another rejection!

n December 26, yes that was Boxing Day, I sent out the event email and had to highlight e fact that only the first 40 who registered would be able to attend. In that google sheet, I d added the steering committee for visibility. In under 3 minutes, the spreadsheet was ghting up like a Christmas tree and we had an additional 50 registered in the waiting list ction. I received emails from many women on the wait list asking if we were able to crease capacity to the event. The executives on the email thread saw the inquiries, and for e first time ever, I did not have to make a formal ask - instead, we were moved to a larger om in order to accommodate the larger group. The event was a huge success - this is when I realized the power of a collective voice to influence a change! We called the event "Women Who Inspire".

A few days later, my mentor found me another opportunity to speak at a conference. It turned out that most of the speakers at the event were men, a fact that did not seem to resonate too well with a lot of the attendees. Feedback was taken in good stride, and it was indeed great to see that at the next conference, many underrepresented groups, including women were selected to present.

This is what inspired me to start a group we later called "SHE" (Sharing Her Empowerment). The goal of the group was to be a change agent through a collective voice. I reached out to a VP who had an amazing background, and she guided me on how to get it started. The name of this chapter and the mission were created by the committee leaders.

The journey of SHE has been simply amazing! We have had the opportunity to raise a lot of awareness, not only at the employee level, but also at the board, and even externally as far as Venture Capitalists. Often diversity is a topic that is handled by HR and employee resource groups. Unfortunately, the number of women represented at the C-suite level is still exceptionally low - at the current 1% per year rate, it will take us into 2050 before we see parity! Laws have been implemented and while some acknowledge that legislation can lead to progress, it does not address the root cause of lack of gender diversity in company leadership and on boards.

One of my goals has always been to be on a board of directors. My mentor introduced me to an executive who said they would be able to help with this. During our conversation, the executive discouraged me, and he told me that I needed more experience.

For a long time, our industry leaders believed that some of the reason why women are not in leadership or board positions are:

1- Lack of ambition
2- Lack of confidence, or
3- Simply not qualified!

Please remember that at times when you "show your hand" (by being ambitious or confident), often you may not be supported, you may be discouraged, and you may not get what you wanted.

With all the breaches today, I feel boards genuinely need individuals with cybersecurity backgrounds, and this is what led me to start up a company called Standout To Lead. The mission is to inspire women in cybersecurity to get onto boards. My first workshop didn't go as expected. As I began advertising to my network, I realized that it's not easy to get a room full of women together. I received many excuses:

1) I am working and I can't get time off.
2) It is too expensive.
3) I'll think about it at a later stage in my career.

For every answer that was a no, I had an answer with an offer to help. I even created a justification case so that their organization would pay for the fees and it worked! This was hard but I knew that this was the first step to making a change. My next workshop was easier as I managed to get a corporate sponsor and sold out the seats quickly.

I've always asked many interviewers and leaders why they don't have equal or diverse representation on their board or on their Executive Leadership team. The most common answer is that we have tried but we are not getting a response. In my opinion, that's not good enough because what I've seen is that there is an unconscious bias during the recruitment process and underrepresented groups aren't given an opportunity. We need to build allies and help them see through our lens and the best way is to challenge them to expand their search and hire based on potential.

We've seen through this pandemic that working remotely is clearly possible. Recently a leader couldn't continue a conversation with regards to a career path with me because of my location. I questioned him – WHY? If location is brought up as a barrier, I encourage you to speak up and if they still can't hire or promote you because of an excuse, it probably isn't a company you would want to work for! Work from Anywhere with flexible hours needs to be the new norm to attract a diverse talent.

My final piece of advice is that I ask you to join us - together we will break boundaries, systemic barriers and be part of an exciting journey where change is taking place. I joined the OWASP Vancouver board to recruit women at our meetups and increase female speakers. Gender diversity was a focus and this year, I am proud to share that we have 50% gender equality on our board. We also increased the number of female speakers and coached them as they prepared for their talks. I also joined ISACA Vancouver She Leads Tech board to build partnerships and allies.

During the pandemic as events became virtual, people started noticing many panels were "manels". We saw on social media leaders influencing a change by not registering for webinars where there wasn't an equal gender or diverse representation.

That inspired me to find a way to influence a similar change at external conferences and felt it was time for me to lead by example by submitting talks. At first, internal teams were concerned because the assumption was that I may not be credible due to having a title as a sales professional.

Luckily, as I was already presenting my own webinars it helped me justify internally and I received support but now I needed to handle the next battle – "Rejection"! I've heard statements from conference organisers that there aren't enough submissions from women. The reality is that when we do submit, our talks are not selected.

My talk on "There is No Security Skills Shortage" didn't get accepted at my first submission but that didn't stop me as I submitted it to other conferences. I also submitted topics on "Breaking Boundaries – Influencing a change through SHE". I was determined and kept submitting to local and national conferences. It worked! Finally, two conferences accepted the topic, which gave me the opportunity to invite other female speakers to present with me.

Our presentations inspired many individuals to consider presenting at future events. In fact, one of our topics was the most viewed on BSides Calgary YouTube channel!

In 2020, I was humbled to receive an Honoree Award by WISECRA and ITWorld Canada and was nominated as one of the top 20 Cybersecurity Women in Canada. I was the only sales professional to receive an award and I believe this will encourage other women in cyber sales to seek nominations in the future.

However, getting to that point had been an uphill battle. I remember reaching out to a leader who I thought knew my potential and asked him to nominate me for the award. Unfortunately, I was given several excuses, and, in the end, was not nominated by him. It sounds unbelievable but it is true. In the end, not receiving his nomination didn't make a difference as I still received the honoree award.

As they say, "Actions speak louder than words". A leader reached out to me and said he is all about diversity and wants to get involved to accelerate SHE initiative within the organization. I offered him a position on our SHE leadership team, and he gave all sorts of excuses. So, I offered him a small task instead and to provide his findings at our next meetup. Each one of the meetups he provided an excuse that he couldn't make the meetup. Being an ally does not mean saying the right things to look good or creating a statement on the website or putting up pictures of diverse groups. Being an ally means taking action and leading with intention by promoting within, lifting underrepresented groups, and speaking up when you or someone has an unconscious bias or expresses sexism and microaggression.

Rome wasn't built in a day! We cannot close the gap overnight but with every one of us speaking up and doing our part, it will happen over time, but it will take each and every one of us or it won't happen at all. I wish what I know now I knew 20 years ago - while I cannot change my past, I now have the courage to speak up for equality, be a voice and pay it forward.

To summarize here are my 5 tips and advice:

1- Be authentic, speak up for equality and don't be afraid of the outcome.
2- Many of us have studied a completely different course and landed into cybersecurity. We are applying our soft skills into our cybersecurity roles. If the adversary has no barriers to entry, why should we?
3- Don't let anyone tell you that you are not good enough. Life is like a *"Safari"* of experiences and everyone has their own path.
4- Take the time to find a mentor and a sponsor and pay it forward.
5- Join us and be part of an exciting journey where change is taking place. Together we will break down barriers and boundaries to achieve equality and pave the path for future generations. A great quote from Ruth Bader Ginsburg that I like to quote is *"Fight for the things you care about. But do it in a way that will lead others to join you"*.

"Gender Diversity should not be a woman's problem to solve, or an HR issue to handle - nor a legislation to be implemented, or a movement to occur... it should be everybody's problem to solve!"

Aarti Gadhia

Asante, Shukriya, Merci, Arigato Gozaimasu, and Thank You for allowing me to share my journey.

Chapter 14

Name: Jacinda Erkelens

Job Title: Information Assurance Specialist

Company: Telstra

Location: Canberra, Australia

How it started

From a young age, I knew I would be working in an exciting industry. I believe this stemmed from a conversation I had with my Dad when I was five, being driven to or from Video Ezy. It went something like this:

Dad: "Do you like Dad's cars?"
Me: "Yes"
Dad: "Do you like that I can buy you all the video from the store you like?"
Me: "Yes."
Dad: "Do you like I can buy you all the clothes you want?"
Me: "Yes."
Dad: "Well, if you like this lifestyle, you will need to study hard and find a good job you love, which will enable you maintain this lifestyle."

I took my dad's advice on studying hard but was too young to consider what my job would be 20 years later. My parents encouraged me to go into a new industry and I started my Bachelor of Security Studies at university right after high school. At the time I knew cyber security was a career option, but it was not top of the list for two reasons. Firstly, the intelligence and counter terrorism-based careers looked the most appealing. Secondly, due to my father's career in the IT project/program management space, and being a Maroon 5 fan, I was concerned going down the cyber route would result in the assumption "…you say that you made it on your own when you haven't worked for anyone your daddy didn't know" and being someone who likes to stand on my own merit, this notion did not sit well with me.

When I was doing my elective units in politics and missing security so much, I agreed to put my name down for a cyber security challenge with a few friends. One of the requirements was that the team must have a mentor with cyber security, IT academic or industry experience. Given my father's background, I put him down. That evening over dinner I explained I had put his contact details down, which is why he would be getting emails, and there was no expectation for him to contribute. However, he did get involved, assisting with our reports and speeches ahead of the two-day competition. As the competition progressed, r team was the only undergraduate team in the finals, and we were awarded for having me of the best documentation.

ike to tell this story for a few reasons.

- It was very much my turning point for myself. A policy role in cyber security became the ost appealing.
- It gave me a newfound appreciation of my father and the type of support he could offer om a personal development perspective. I also noticed throughout the competition, no one ew who my father was, which broke down my internal barrier about standing on my own o feet.
- This was the first of many opportunities I took to enhance my experience in cyber curity, as unfortunately opportunities were scarce at university.

ollowing this challenge, I competed in more hackathons, competitions, industry onferences, summits, and other events. These gave me glimpses into the who and what ber security is all about, and the networking was invaluable. Some of my favourite emories include eating a Mars Bar at 11pm learning about the Graduate Program portunities with AUSTRAC, and encouraging my introverted peers in networking at an ISA conference, which resulted in one obtaining 3kg of swag!

uring these events, I didn't take note of how few women there were in the room. I was so cited to be there, meet new people, and better my understanding of the cyber security ommunity. I'd come to note over the following years that there are less women than men at ese events, but sadly, our industry isn't as diverse as it could be.

reaking into the industry – My Path, Challenges, and Assumptions

ath

s someone who was studying full time and had limited work experience, a graduate ogram was the logical next step in my career. Due to my background and interests, I cused on cyber risk, project management, security, and general graduate programs. I was termined to get a graduate role, ideally in cyber security.

hallenges

here's a widespread assumption that cyber security is purely technical. One of the more nusual recruitment processes I went through was for a cyber risk role at a large company at has a good reputation for their cyber capabilities. I was successful in the initial pplication, aptitude test and a phone interview. During the phone interview I answered the eneral interview questions, and more specific ones around some of the hackathons I had ompeted in. At the conclusion of the call, it was explained the hackathons intrigued them ough to push my name to the phone interview, but my degree could stop me progressing. I as told to expect a call the following week with an outcome from the HR lead. This call me after the expected timeframe, so naturally I was prepared for an 'unfortunately we will t be progressing with your application'. My hunch was correct, but the wording was quite fferent. It started with the question, 'Why did you apply?', which I answered, touching on the reputation of the organisation, their cyber security capabilities, and opportunities with the organisation. This was followed by a statement, 'Do you know it was inappropriate for you to even apply for this role; we are only interested in IT and software engineering degrees.' Stunned, I asked her to repeat the statement. Given their advertising called for IT, software engineering, cyber security, and similar degrees, I kindly suggested they might update their recruitment materials and left it there.

Whilst it annoyed me for a day or so, I didn't get the chance to mull over it until a little later when I happened to be with my uni peers. I explained to them what had happened and there were two responses. The first was from those who had already interned at that company, and they weren't surprised by my experience. The second response was from someone who had also applied for the same position as me, and after being offered the role, had declined it. This person was after a more technical role and mentioned to the company I would be a better fit. While this did provide a level of entertainment, it opened a window of realisation for me. Cyber security has a vast range of roles and subsequent skillsets; not all are technical. We need to think broadly about skillsets that will add value to cyber security. Since then, I've been much more conscious of the breadth of cyber security and seek to actively dispel myths about the nature of cyber security.

(Incorrect) Assumptions

I got more graduate program offers because of my gender. I recall one afternoon at uni when we were prepping for the cyber security challenge CySCA. The guys in the room claimed I was finding it easy to get job offers due to my gender. I asked the guy who brought up this conversation to tell me how many roles he had applied for. He responded saying about six or seven. I had applied for more than thirty roles by this point. So, when you do the math, the reason I had five times the number of offers he did was most likely due to the volume of applications I had made, not my gender. I could not help but recall one of my initial hesitations associated with cyber security – justifying how I obtained my role. This type of experience I also feel is not unique to myself.

By the time my university journey had come to an end, I had submitted 40 plus graduate program applications, attended dozens of interviews, and received a few offers. I have joined the industry through an adjacent academic background, which based on the requirements of graduate programs, is not considered linear. After reviewing the offers I did receive, I chose to join Telstra as a cyber security graduate. The breadth of cyber security opportunities in non-technical roles and the attitude towards my degree during the recruitment process made it an incredibly appealing choice.

My first days

After my two days of general graduate induction training, I was still unsure of what specifically my team did, or what I should wear, noting my first day with my team was a Friday and I knew first impressions were crucial. At 6:45am I was almost ready to begin my 2-hour commute to the Sydney office. Before I left, Mum gave me a hug, and my Dad handed me a phone charging cable, Crunchie chocolate bar, and flip flops. When I entered the office and got to meet the team, I was delighted and intrigued to discover half the team were women. During my first team meeting everyone introduced themselves and I learnt why the team was so diverse - each person had taken different paths into the world of third-party security vendor and solutions assessments. For the women, it was accounting, IT and coding backgrounds. On many occasions during my rotation with the team, I appreciated how insightful they were and how their backgrounds added incredible value to the world of third-party security assessments, whether that be answering a quick question I had or a general appreciation for adjacent skills.

When I commenced my second rotation, I discovered my new team was closer to what is more commonly seen in the industry – just 12% women. While I do not feel being in a heavily male dominated area is a negative thing in the context of performing taskings and completing projects, of course there are some observations – and some are quite amusing. One instance was when I finally found a pair of work pants with pockets, and pre-caffeinated me was so happy I had to tell the whole office I had pockets. Of course, the only person who shared my excitement was the other female present as the males didn't realise women's workwear rarely has pockets. I've also had a few occasions when I'm looking at a meeting invite list and realise, I'm the only female invited. I feel badass, and a little lonely at the same time. However, it is worth noting, that says more about STEM than cyber security itself.

My work dad

In high school there was one friend who shared the same passion for all thing's security. At 17, we would joke we would end up as work husband and wife, follow each other's career successes on LinkedIn, and recommend each other for jobs. However, this is not how things have shaped out. I have ended up with a work dad.

My work dad has the same attributes as a mentor, but as someone I worked for and with, and knowing some of the more personal aspects of my life, he is a unique support person in my career and personal development. His name is Alan. He works for the team I completed my first rotation in. As he is based in Tasmania, the first time I saw him was online during a team meeting. About a month after I joined, he gave me and the other new starters a security assessment to do; we all took one vendor each and were given a week to review and send him our findings. I remember warning Alan my report resembles a rainbow. During a subsequent call to explain my findings, and the logic associated with the rainbows, he told me he liked the way I worked, and wanted to know if I would work alongside him for one of the largest projects the team had. This was the beginning of daily calls, regular debriefs and significant development as Alan took me along this journey, and even had me behind the steering wheel while he went on a well-deserved holiday. He taught me everything he knew, and then some.

A few months after I had left the team, my mum and I were holidaying in Tasmania and we met up with Alan. On one occasion my mum mentioned I considered Alan my work dad (which was not new to him), and my line manager as my work mum. Alan's wife had a good giggle while explaining she called our line manager Alan's work wife – so everyone within our own biological families considered the three of us a little work family! I always thought I'd meet some amazing people in the workplace, but my expectations have been far surpassed. Not only have I met amazing people, but I've built great friendships with them.

The percentage of women in cyber security is low: How not to deal with it.

I think it's generally agreed that overall, the level of female participation in the cyber security industry is low. There have been many occasions where the 'why' of these low numbers have been discussed – as they should be. Acknowledging there is a problem is the first step in recovery, which can be applied in this context. While this topic is generally received with nothing but positivity and ideas, there are less than ideal ways to address the low number of women in the field.

One which will always stand out to me is a more adverse reaction I had when I presented my observations on the why female participation in cyber security is low. It occurred after I had recently moved to Canberra, so I'd been working in the field for about a year. I had some experience, but not a whole lot. I was listening to a presentation and I'd written some notes on their rhetorical questions about getting more women into cyber security. The presenters were friendly and seemed to genuinely want more insights for their research, so I approached them afterwards and shared my experiences with them. While I didn't expect anything more than acknowledgement of the words coming out of my mouth, I didn't expect the response I got. I shared that my university cohort dropped from 60% women to 25% women after just one tutorial – a tutorial in which we were told it was not an industry for women if you wanted to have both a family and a career. The speakers were shocked that this conversation was happening in universities as the reality is quite different; the speakers themselves were women juggling both a family and a career in cyber, and proof it was possible. They didn't quite believe that conversations about flexibility (or lack thereof) in the workplace were happening so early at university when career choices were being made. I was disappointed they didn't take on board this observation, as there is huge potential to increase the participation rates of women in the field if we're showing that flexibility does exist and what's possible. I know there are companies which have great flexible environments and enable women to bring their whole selves to work and achieve in their career whilst also having a family – Telstra is evidence of that! We need to be correcting the conversations happening in the university setting, and not dispel such observations when shared with those doing research to improve diversity.

There are also two instances I recall where the numbers around female participation were, in my opinion, fudged.

The first one occurred during a summit, where one company was boasting they had reached a 25% female participation rate, and the number was rising. As a female student, I was keen to understand how they had achieved this – was it a quota, a hiring policy, something within this company's culture which appeals to women (e.g. flexibility, or parental leave policy), or through a university program? Or was it a combination? I was not the only one with this question. During the next available break, I was one of four people who asked the speakers about this. Their answer was that their data included the privacy and legal teams which were female dominated. Now this could be a valid data set – cyber security teams come in all shapes and sizes, so including privacy and legal in the GRC space does make sense from a skill set perspective. One person followed up asking if these teams are specifically assigned to cyber security. The answer was no, and they proceeded to explain only one or two people rom each team would be assigned to cyber security tasks when required. So that begged the question – what is the percentage of women working in cyber security roles, or roles primarily dedicated to cyber security tasks or projects?

The second instance was at a cyber security competition, the following month. It was a small competition of about 40 participants, and you had to apply (and be accepted) to compete. At the end of the competition, the event organisers requested a photo of all competitors, which isn't unusual. But what was unusual was that they asked the female volunteers to be in the photo too. We were moved around to try and 'even things out' for the photo, and it was uncomfortable and there was confusion about why it was happening. By including these additional women, it gave the impression that 15% of the competitors were women, instead of accurate 7.5%. I saw the photo circulated after the event on numerous social media accounts – again this is not unusual, but with the captions noting the diversity, I could not help but cringe.

These tactics can be considered 'quick wins' from a business perspective by boosting numbers, and hoping this boost encourages other women to apply at these companies. It seems to be smoke and mirrors for me. These tactics also don't look to understand or address the underlying reason/s there are less women in the industry. It's great to have conversations about the percentage of females in cyber security, but let's be truthful about the data so we can have an honest conversation and show true progress.

Bucking the trend with children

While we're yet to have enough people to meet the demand for cyber security skills, it's incredible to see children pick up cyber security skills at such a young age. I volunteer at cyber security events for primary school aged children, and seeing the children compete in challenges and do incredibly well is one of the most rewarding parts of working in cyber. The events I have been a part of have seen an even mix of males and females participate, especially if it has been part of a school's STEM day. With prizes on the line (generally a drone for 1st place) and usernames not indicating who the participant is, it is the points and accuracy scores which determine who is winning. Mentors have a better visibility over how far the kids have progressed in the challenges because they are the people on standby to guide the kids through the challenges when they get stuck. From a skills perspective there is zero difference between boys and girls. It's brilliant to see both boys and girls take out first place – and the only advantage any child would have, it seems, is if their parent or carer works in cyber security and therefore the child has had greater exposure to the required skills and techniques.

Final thoughts

I've only been in the industry a relatively short period of time, but if the observations I have made throughout my journey are a true representation of the cyber security landscape in Australia, it begs asking questions. Why is the reduction in diversity so significant between primary school and the workforce? What factors influence the journey along the way? What can we do to address it? Are the many existing initiatives to improve diversity in the workforce creating change? How long will it take to get to a 50/50 representation, or dare I say, a female dominated profession?

I think big and know I can act local. My hope is that the children who are taking part in cyber challenges see a diverse group of mentors and know it's a profession in which they'd be welcome. My hope is that we knock down the rumours that abound in education settings about our profession and make sure people know that many different opportunities exist in cyber, and that it's not a choice between family or career. My hope is that we foster a workplace where everyone can contribute – because if we're to beat our adversary and out-think criminals, we need everyone.

Chapter 15

Name: Kim Crawley

Job Title: Cybersecurity researcher and author

Company: AT&T Cybersecurity

Location: Toronto, Canada

Due to my undiagnosed autism and ADHD, I really struggled in school when I was 10 years old in 1994. My brain can handle arithmetic just fine. But the emotional trauma of constant bullying had a detrimental effect on my school performance. Plus, I have an unconventional way of solving division problems. The school system didn't care. It didn't matter that I could get the correct answer without cheating, if my steps differed from the textbook then I got no marks.

Noting the year is important, because it was a time when personal computer use was exploding, but most households had yet to use the internet. My teacher noticed my early interest in computers. In her twisted mind, she thought saying the following would motivate me to improve my math grades: "Kimberly, if you want to work with computers when you grow up, you must be a math whiz!"

At age 36, I'm still furious that she thought my problem was a lack of motivation. And of course, her inaccurate advice had an effect she certainly didn't intend-- instead of my grades improving, I gave up on the idea of pursuing a computing career. I also dropped out of high school at age 16 because the years of intense emotional trauma had taken their toll. Looking back, I'm surprised that I didn't try to kill myself.

When I was 14, I discovered what ADHD was on the web. I insisted that my parents help me seek diagnosis and hoped it would mean that I finally received proper support in school. My parents reluctantly took me to a specialist, and then they answered their questionnaires in a way to deliberately deny me diagnosis. They couldn't live with the shame, which was more important than my well-being.

Around the same time, my teacher suspected I was autistic. Unbeknownst to me at the time, a supposed specialist visited the classroom to just observe me while I was in class with the other kids. I made eye contact, so my opportunity to be diagnosed was denied! I found out about this during a parent-teacher meeting a few months later. Of course, my teacher spoke to my parents as if I weren't in the room. It infuriates me how disrespected I was. Children deserve to be spoken with directly when it comes to whether or not they're being diagnosed with a neurological condition. But children are subhuman to these abusive adults.

As I got older, I learned that computer programmers and IT professionals usually *aren't* math geniuses. By my mid-20s, I got a CompTIA A+ and Network+. With that, I got a job as a remote desktop support technician. Around the same time, I wrote my high school equivalency exam. The exam didn't care which steps I took to solve math problems, as long as I didn't cheat. To my surprise, I aced the math component!

When I worked in remote support, I would typically close about thirty tickets per day. This was around 2007 to 2008. Most of those tickets had malware-related issues. I probably removed malware from thousands of Windows machines. Then sometimes I would need to fix the damage that the malware caused. For instance, I had to write Windows Registry keys sometimes. I even saw ransomware that predated cryptocurrency. Back in 2007, ransomware demanded credit card numbers! All that work made me catch the cybersecurity bug.

I spent several years researching and writing about cybersecurity issues on the web. By 2017, I was able to make enough money from cybersecurity blogging for it to be my full-time job. My first major break was with Tripwire's State of Security blog. From there, I got gigs contributing to Sophos' Naked Security, Venafi's blog, BlackBerry Cylance's ThreatVector, and many others. I started contributing to AlienVault's blog in 2017. I kept contributing when AT&T bought the company and rebranded it AT&T Cybersecurity. I still contribute to AT&T Cybersecurity's blog today.

In Canada, adult autism and ADHD diagnosis isn't covered under our public healthcare system. When I was poor, I couldn't seek any help. But my cybersecurity blogging career rescued me from poverty as I started to make good money.

In January 2019, at age 35, I spent nearly $3,000 or my own money on the services of an autism diagnosis centre. After days of testing, I was not only diagnosed with autism, but also ADHD inattentive type. My jaw dropped.

Formally diagnosed autistic children are usually subjected to ABA, Applied Behavioural Analysis. ABA is strongly based on gay conversion "therapy," and it's at least equally harmful. Punishing children for not hiding their autistic traits and taking away their teddy bear or food if they don't comply leads to lifelong PTSD. Not only does ABA emotionally traumatize children, but it also teaches children that their bodies don't belong to them and they should never say no to an adult. It makes them ripe for exploitation by rapists and other child abusers. It infuriates me that the Ontario government in Canada pays for it.

I was diagnosed as an adult. An adult who has the legal right to say no. So, there were no "services" for me. The only support for autistic adults is between ourselves, in our communities online. Hopefully one day autistic people will be accepted and embraced for being autistic, while receiving the needed support that *we* ask for. The greatest harm done to disabled people is that abled people decide what's best for us, to our tremendous detriment. Abled people dominate our narrative. We disabled people must control our narrative and our destinies instead. "Nothing about us without us."

The COVID19 pandemic has transformed my career. Big tech companies cut their marketing budgets. The only corporate blog I still contribute to is AT&T's. But that terrible year brought wonderful opportunities to me.

My reputation led to a lot of threat intel research gigs behind the scenes. And in April 2020, my friend, pentester Phillip Wylie asked me to cowrite his book, The Pentester Blueprint. It was published by Wiley Tech (no relation!) in November 2020.

The book got a strongly positive response in both sales and Twitter hype. Thanks to the opportunity Phil and Wiley gave me, I was able to sign a new book deal with the publisher in December 2020. This time, I'm writing the book on my own. But Phil and I enjoyed our collaboration, and we may work together again in the future. I'm also exploring the idea of writing titles for O'Reilly Media. And the threat intel gigs keep coming in.

I don't have any specific advice for women in cybersecurity other than to persevere and believe in yourself. I faced a lot of struggle and hardship to get where I am. But now I enjoy a wonderful career and I learn something new about cybersecurity every day.

Your destiny isn't completely within your control. We human beings are interdependent; we rely on each other. But you can do your part and improve your odds by never giving up.

I believe in you!

Chapter 16

Name: Deborah Leary, OBE, D.Univ, FRSA

Job Title: CEO

Company: Forensic Pathways Ltd/Clarifyi.com

Location: Birmingham, UK

If there is one lesson I have learnt in my somewhat advanced years is that life tends to come full circle, that every experience has a value whether it is good, bad, or indifferent, and that whilst those experiences may not feel connected, they ultimately are because they are the essence of the person you become and the building blocks of the resilience you need.

My journey into Cyber is definitely unconventional, but on reflection, looking at all the small events that made up my life to this point, to me it seems a natural step. As I take you on just a small piece of my journey, I hope to share some lessons I've learnt. The first one is within the opening paragraph of this Chapter.

Lesson 1: There is a value in every experience – experience builds resilience.
I consider myself a good generalist and opportunist, all of which stems from being extremely curious. I've learnt to know what I'm not good at and these are invariably the things I don't enjoy doing or don't have the skill base for, nor never will because the detail of it doesn't spark me into action.

So how did Debbie Holloway, a child born in the 60's in Birmingham end up starting a company that now works within cyber? It wasn't the plan.

considered myself a consistently average child with a passion for dancing, reading, and a error of getting into trouble. My start was slightly hampered by a speech impediment till I was around 6 years which made me at times undecipherable. At the time it seemed a curse, but in later years I came to see it as a blessing as it made me realise the power of communication, something I shall come back to later in this Chapter. So, there I was with a speech impediment, second teeth that were too big for my face with a gap you could drive a truck through and nowhere to hide. No avatar to take the pressure off. What it did provide was an ability to live off wit.

Lesson 2: Laughter is power – Laughter is a leveller.

Having survived school fairly unscathed, mainly through being Head Librarian, hiding in the Library and being a Prefect protected by a red sash to denote my authority, the fateful day arrived when I was summoned to the Library to meet with the Careers Teacher (a man wearing a hacking jacket with patches on the elbow and sporting an unkempt beard). This was a defining moment. Having asked me what I wanted to be and getting the reply 'a photographic journalist', his response was 'what about nursing or the civil service'. Even at 14 I swiftly realised that here was someone whose horizons were somewhat limited. From that conversation with the Careers Teacher, I looked at my options. I was top of the school at typing and shorthand and all things commerce and knew that I would always have work if I continued to develop in that area and so I went to Technology College to undertake a London Chamber of Commerce Private Secretaries Certificate, along with 2 A Levels in English and Law.

I always blamed that Careers Teacher for me not becoming the photographic journalist I dreamt of being and bless my parents, they didn't know what to do, they just loved me, so guidance was limited. It took me years later to realise it wasn't his fault, it was mine. It was just a dream. If I had wanted it badly enough, I would have taken action, I would have found a way, I would have taken steps towards my goal. In any event, life has taken me to many places, so photography has played a big part in my life.

Lesson 3: Goals need action.

Having completed my course I began my career as a PA, working for a criminal lawyer which he in fact turned out to be himself – a whole chapter could be devoted to this), a shorthand typist at West Midlands Police (at which point I asked to apply to join the Police but was told I was too short), then as a PA to the Local Radio Officer at the Independent Broadcasting Authority and so it continued with a variety of secretarial jobs until 2001.

I had been working in a Secondary School and Sixth Form as an Office/Training Manager at the same time completing my English Language and Literature degree at what was then the University of Central England, now Birmingham City University. Married, with two small children and a full-time job, the course had to be part-time taking 5 years to complete. The plan was that I complete the degree and work my way into becoming a university lecturer, a writer of books and articles. An academic. I had covered so much in my degree from Shakespeare, to 10th Century English, to crime novels, the plays of David Mamet and Jane

Austin, but nothing captured my imagine more than the science fiction element of the course, studying Cyberpunk[1], Mary Shelley, Marge Piercy, and William Gibson[2]. Studying the theories of Cyborg Politics/the body politic I focussed on what it means to be human and how the symbiosis between human and machine will affect our response to humanity. I studied theorists such as Donna Haraway, and researched cybernetics, thanks to my introduction to Professor Kevin Warwick[3], author of 'The March of the Machines: The Breakthrough in Artificial Intelligence, formerly Professor of Cybernetics at the University of Reading and now a Professor at Coventry University.

Having completed my degree, I decided to undertake my Masters. The grandiose title for my MA was 'The future impact on gender and identity through the increased use of bio and communications technology as highlighted in the works of William Gibson, Marge Piercy, Mary Shelley and Donna Haraway. I never finished the MA because …

Then came Toronto – Part 1 of my journey – crime scene.
In March 2001, my husband, who was a West Midlands Police Officer, was invited to speak at a Police Conference in Toronto to present on research he was conducting for his PhD in Law and Evidence. At that same time, I had secured myself my first teaching job at a local college and had three weeks free before I started my new job, therefore the invite to tag along on the trip to Toronto to have a holiday and enjoy my photography was quickly taken up.

As with most international conferences, the night before the conference a welcome reception was held for people to mingle and generally network. I have to admit I was initially reluctant to attend as I believed I had nothing to offer in terms of comment or expertise. However, thankfully I was persuaded to attend and as a consequence my interest was raised so much so that the following day, I decided to attend the opening of the conference and forego a city tour.

At this point in the story people often ask what inspired me at the conference and in the end, what led to follow the path I have subsequently taken. This is a question I've often pondered and have come to the simple conclusion that this was the first time in my life where I hadn't got an agenda. There was little point in my being there and as a consequence my mind was open and relaxed, unclouded from the noise that usually fills our heads when we are normally rushing about our daily tasks.

---

[1] https://en.wikipedia.org/wiki/Cyberpunk

[2] https://williamgibson.fandom.com/wiki/Sprawl_trilogy. 1984 – 1988 Trilogy - Gibson focuses on the effects of technology: the unintended consequences. He explores a world of direct mind-machine links ("jacking in"), emerging machine intelligence, and a global information space which he calls "cyberspace". Some of the novels' action takes places in The Sprawl, an urban environment that extends along much of the east coast of the US.

[3] https://www.coventry.ac.uk/research/researchers/professor-kevin-warwick/

Lesson 4: Stepping back brings clarity.

The keynote speaker for the Conference was the one and only Dr Henry Lee, a key figure in the O.J. Simpson Case and being naturally curious the first day of the conference I joined the throng of others keen to get an insight into the events of the case. Henry described at length (with photos) the scene and its management. Unbeknown to me this was the start of my journey that was to follow for at that precise point I realised that all I had learnt through my English Degree; the construction of narrative, was exactly the process experienced by an investigator when attending a crime scene, with the exception that the investigator was in the unique position of being both the reader of the scene and the author of the narrative. From this point I began to construct an outline for a paper entitled 'The Art of Storytelling in Police Investigation'. However, it was later in the bar (where all the best stories and deals are made) that one of the most important actions I have ever taken occurred and which has been the catalyst for everything that has happened since. Sitting in the bar listening (not participating, I knew nothing about the forensic world apart from reading crime scene novels as part of my degree) I listened to investigators from different countries talking about their jobs, the difficulties faced, the procedures they followed and the equipment they used. During the course of the conversation an officer from the UK mentioned the use of a piece of equipment known as a 'stepping plate'. Immediately the Canadian officer in the group said they hadn't heard of that equipment or approach and a discussion ensued. At this precise moment I scribbled on a scrap of Colony Hotel notepaper I had been using to take notes, three things:

find out about stepping plates/shoes.
found open market.
Set up Co.

To this day I don't know why I did it, but something said to me here was an opportunity. Stepping Plates are low level platforms which come in a couple of sizes, the most popular being 350 x 350 and they are placed down at a crime scene so that investigators can walk and work within the scene without contaminating or damaging evidence. Basically, they are steppingstones.

Arriving back in the UK I started my new teaching role but wasn't prepared to leave behind the idea of supplying Stepping Plates to Canada as a sideline to earn extra income. Arranged by my long-suffering husband I turned up at a local police station to collect a Stepping Plate. I thought it would be a piece of scientific equipment designed specifically to address a need. It wasn't. The Stepping Plate was made from aluminium treadplate, which had a wide lip that ran underneath so that it would balance on the floor. It was heavy, unstackable, clearly difficult to clean, would skid when used on laminate flooring, but most importantly of all it wasn't transparent. **Question.** How can you construct what has happened at a crime scene, note points of potential entry and exit, see evidence on the floor, if it is covered with aluminium? It was clear that this was a reaction to a need rather than a proactive design. Surely there were other styles available?

I therefore did what we were all doing back in 2001. I cranked up the internet on dial up, made a cup of tea whilst it loaded and then began a search for a transparent Stepping Plate. They didn't exist.

Often when I speak to people about how I started they say the eureka moment must have come when I wrote the note on the hotel note paper, or when I cranked up the computer and realised that there was the opportunity to invent something new. In fact, I don't believe either of these can be considered a eureka moment. That came later on a grey day travelling back to Birmingham from Liverpool.

A company who had been exhibiting at the conference in Canada was based in Liverpool and they made laboratory equipment (predominantly plastic). My simplistic view of how my life was going to be was that I would travel to Liverpool, clutching a confidentiality agreement I had downloaded from the internet, tell them my idea of creating a transparent, lightweight stackable Stepping Plate, they would make it and I would simply have a royalty from any sales they made. My life would continue as planned, writing papers/books and lecturing. Having explained what I needed they politely informed me that what I needed was to speak to someone involved in plastic injection moulding and pointed me in the direction of a couple of contacts who they thought could help me get tooling made (at this point I didn't know what plastic injection moulding was, nor what they meant by tooling). I got in my car and headed back down the M6. And here it comes – the EUREKA moment.... I rang my husband and naturally he asked me how things had gone. I said 'Yes, it's gone good, but the only way this is going to happen is if I take control of it – I'm going to set up a company. I've thought of the name – it's Forensic Pathways.' **EUREKA!**

Lesson 5: If you want Eureka you have to take action and you have to take responsibility. No action, no responsibility = #noughtbutadream.
On the 11 July 2001 Forensic Pathways Ltd came into being, at least on paper. I continued to work in teaching and in my spare time spoke with a variety of police forces to get feedback on my idea. I sent out the world's worst marketing material to every police force in the country with a mock-up of a transparent Stepping Plate and one Thursday afternoon my mobile rang and it was a police force asking to buy the Plates. Telling someone that something doesn't exist despite the fact that you've sent them out marketing was always going to be a tumbleweed moment, but I said that there was no point me investing time and money if the market didn't want it and now that they had called, I had proof that they did. I asked them to be patient and that I would deliver in a year. Bless them they did, and they have been clients ever since.

I subsequently spent 2001 – 2003 designing the world's first transparent Stepping Plate, cajoling people to help. In fact, the quote for the first tools came in at £250,000. When the guys told me, I laughed and said that I only had my family allowance and my teaching salary so they needed to do better. Whilst they were scratching their heads, I managed to get a SMART Award for a prototype. Eventually the guys came back and told me they could get the tooling from China for £60,000. Armed with a business plan I got a business loan from a high street bank for £60k and in the first week of January 2003 moved into an office, just me a telephone and fax machine, waiting on a slow boat from China to land with my tooling. The first order for Plates came via fax around May 2003 from the National Police Training College, for which I shall be forever grateful. The rest as they say is history, with a few bumps along the road, but an incredible product success now sold all over the world, forming part of Standard Operating Procedures for the UK/Europe. Recently it has been fantastic to see them being used in action on the first episode of BBC2's latest documentary - Forensics: The Real CSI. It makes everything worthwhile when you see an idea making a positive impact.

The Stepping Plates have also featured in iconic shows such as Silent Witness, Vera, and CSI New York, which I had the pleasure of going to see being filmed in LA (if you want to see the episode with the Stepping Plates featured it is the episode titled 'Boo'). I should also say thanks to shows like CSI New York as I also began to get calls from Universities, who had recognised the popularity of Forensic Science being driven by these shows and who wanted to offer Forensic Science as a subject for students. Whilst the universities were geared up to do biology, chemistry, and physics, they had no understanding of Forensic Science and crime scene management. As a result, I brought together recently retired investigators, consultants and developed Practical Forensics Courses which we would provide to the Universities during the summer break, training them and advising them on course content prior to the terms starting.

Lesson 6: You don't have to be in forensics to start a forensic company.
Survival in business needs many elements, two of which are innovation and diversification. So, we travel to…

Part 2 of the journey – all things digital
I knew that we couldn't survive on just one product and at the same time I didn't want to just simply be a reseller of other company's products. By 2003 I had a full team including my son Ben Leary, now Director of Forensic Pathways, followed by my husband in 2006. Researching the market is key as is projecting forward. Having recognised that the forensic market was diversifying into digital, with the new commodity being data, we began to develop technology which reflected the changing environment. At every stage of the journey we worked collaboratively with other organisations, police forces and universities globally in order to develop new innovations, particularly in the area of mobile phone data, image analysis and ballistics analysis: Forensic Digital Exchange (FDX) for the management of mobile phone data, Forensic Image Analyser (FIA) for the identification of the unique signature within an image attributing images to devices; Loquitur Ballistics, a ballistics correlation technology.

Throughout this second part of the journey, we became known for having significant skill in developing technologies for data management and analysis and as a result other work began to develop in the area of due diligence and fraud investigation, involving OSINT. Something which has shaped much of the 3rd part of my journey.

Lesson 7: You don't have to be in digital forensics to start a digital forensics company.
I must acknowledge Dr Richard Leary, MBE, my husband who was fundamental to the success of our digital development. Richard had been a senior Police Officer within West Midlands Police. During his service he undertook a PhD in Law and Evidence as a result of which he developed a system called FLINTS (Forensic Led Intelligence System) which until recently had continued to be used by a number of police forces in the UK.[4] Joining Forensic Pathways in 2006 he helped shape our response to the changing world of forensic investigation until his passing in 2015. A supporter of my 'if we build it, they will come' approach.

Reflection: journey so far – crime scene forensics – digital forensics and so to…

Part 3: The Return of the Cyberwoman
Life has a habit of coming full circle. This is why it is important to remember that every experience whether it is good, bad, or indifferent, each has a purpose, bringing you to the point that you are and the person you've become. I don't believe in happy accidents I believe that there is order in what appears to be randomness.

If we return my introduction to this chapter I have always been incredibly interested in cyber, what it means, technologies impact on what it means to be human, how we would communicate in a cyber world where gender and identity is fluid, where on the Net you can be whatever you want to be. This is also a world where words matter. What we say or don't say impacts on politics, economics, security, and livelihoods.

Lesson 8: Words matter, choose them carefully.
An example of why words matter follows. In 1979 I was studying for my A Level English. As part of the course, we had to read The Sandcastle by Iris Murdoch. This book had a profound effect on me. It is ultimately about the breakdown of a marriage. On the first page, three quarters of the way down there is a sentence. 'It was a cold lunch'. Five words that summed up the entire novel. Five words that said it all. It was cold, the marriage was dead. Those five words have stayed with me because they symbolise the impact and importance of communication and of the construction of 'story'. I have been intrigued and passionate about storytelling ever since.

Travel 30 years later.
I've decided that I've been working too much and that I need to see bigger horizons so look for an adventure. My adventure turns into an Everest Base Camp Trek, which involved arriving at Kathmandu, travelling in the smallest plane known to man, landing at the World's most dangerous airport, Lukla, then trekking 9 days to Base Camp and 5 back, sleeping in a

---

[4] https://link.springer.com/chapter/10.1007/978-90-481-8990-8_7
https://www.theguardian.com/technology/2000/feb/03/onlinesupplement9

wo-person tent with someone I didn't know. We were two days from Base Camp and on the way to our next camp when we arrived at a monastery in the middle of the Himalayas. The monastery was closed but we were told that across the vast plain in front of us was an outbuilding in which the Monks had left chocolate, biscuits, and other snacks for walkers to help themselves to on their journey. In the dusk, desperate for some chocolate I set across the field to visit the outbuilding. Scouring the shelves with my nightlight I could see that most of the chocolate was out of date but that wasn't going to stop me. I then saw what I thought was a small box on the top shelf and reached up. Only it wasn't a box. It was a book. The Sandcastle by Iris Murdoch. The only book there. I caught my breath and as if I didn't expect it to be there, I turned to the first page, three quarters down, and read 'It was a cold lunch'. Standing in that vast open space in the middle of the Himalayas' on my own I realised the connectivity of life. That there is a reason for everything and every thought, experience, every word has a value. I didn't take the book. I left it for someone else who I hoped would feel the impact of the words the same way as I did back in 1979.

Lesson 9: Stories matter.

So, what has this got to do with Cyber?

Remember diversification is everything, projecting futures, seizing opportunities, saying yes, and finding the solution. We had been busy developing technology in the digital forensic space, we had adapted to provide due diligence and fraud investigation services using the perfect balance between technology and human intel. Knowing what was out there on the Clear Web was one thing, but just like a David Mamet play it was the silences in the text, the silences created by the actors that said more. As the adage goes 'it's not what you know that will hurt you'. For us, the Dark Web was the silence and we needed to break it. We knew that for many of our business clients they would naturally carry out due diligence when going into M&A deals or recruiting senior executives, that they would spend huge amounts of money on security systems and IP protection, but they were focused on what they knew. Many saw the Dark Web as a place frequented by drug dealers and little else.

The universe has a way of bringing things to the fore when the time is right. As we had begun to look at how we could create innovations to monitor, analyse and alert us to activity on the Dark Web, we were approached by CIFAS, the national fraud database organisation asking us to undertake research on online fraud on the Clear Web and Dark Web. In 2018 we launched the 'Wolves of the Internet Report'[5] in collaboration with CIFAS. By this time, we had developed our Dark Web Search Engine (DSE), had indexed over 40 million urls (and has naturally continued to grow), crawling 24/7, automatically updating the database every four hours, sending alerts to clients, and providing human intel through our team of analysts. In effect shortening the timeframe to detection of compromised data on the Dark Web, enabling businesses to swiftly identify security gaps and mitigate the damage caused by the misuse of exposed data.

Lesson 10: You don't have to be in cyber to start a cyber company.

---

https://clarifyi.com/case-studies/threat-investigation-wolves-of-the-internet/

Throughout its 20-year history Forensic Pathways has adapted and projected the future. One of our challenges has been how can we get our messages out to clients, when you ultimately have a company that covers such a diverse range of products and services from crime scene, through to digital forensics, through to Cyber. For me, the one thing that binds them together is 'story'. Whether it is the murder scene, a burglary, a paedophile case or a security breach, the ultimate truth is that it is about human behaviour, therefore our response can never just be about the 'tech'.

What's the evidence saying to us, what's missing, where are the gaps, how do we bring it together and how do we do that without bringing our own biases to the conclusion?

Applying the theory of 'story' meant that we had to take a hard look at how we were offering our products and services. What was our story? In the autumn of 2020 in the midst of a pandemic we launched Clarifyi.com[6], a brand within Forensic Pathways, providing Cyber Awareness Training; Background Investigations, Brand Protection, Dark Web Monitoring/OSINT and Executive Impersonation, in effect separating these products and services out from the Forensic Pathways website shop window, leaving that to focus predominantly on crime scene and aspects of digital forensics and ballistics analysis. In creating Clarifyi, we affirmed our offering within the cyber arena, making clear our story. I am now delighted that we are Trusted Partners of the West Midlands Cyber Resilience Centre and are also part of their Advisory Board. Cyber is not just about Zeros and Ones, it's not just about the tech. Success comes from understanding and anticipating human behaviour. All the security in the world won't protect you if investment isn't made in people and their behaviour and all the technical investigative skills in the world won't protect you. Understanding people and behaviour, understanding story, coupled with strong technology is I believe where success lies.

At this point I'd like to go back to the common theme of Lessons 6, 7 and 10.

Lesson 6: You don't have to be in forensics to start a forensic company.
Lesson 7: You don't have to be in digital forensics to start a digital forensics company.
Lesson 10: You don't have to be in cyber to start a cyber company.

The Ultimate Lesson
Too often people don't take an opportunity because they 'don't know', 'they've no experience'. They forget to think in the round. They forget all the other skills, knowledge, intuitions they have that have as much relevance. I wasn't a forensic scientist, I didn't have experience in digital forensics, I didn't have experience in cyber. Seeing the opportunity, understanding the problem, building a team with the experience and skills that complement what you do have so you can create the solution, that's the ultimate lesson. Cyber isn't a mystery, it isn't a dark art. It's people and technology, some working for good, some working for bad.

---

[6] https://clarifyi.com/

y journey into cyber was laid out without me even recognising it. It started with my
ssion and curiosity for stories, an interest in the impact of technology on what it means to
human and a belief that good things happen if you embrace change. The story continues, it
ay be good, it may be bad, it may be indifferent, but one thing is for sure things don't go
ong they just go different. It may be cyber now, but what next.

at's my story. What's yours?

Chapter 17

Name: Michala Liavaag

Job Title: Head of Information Security / Cyber Security Lead

Company: None – currently on sabbatical

Location: South East, UK

I'm Michala Liavaag – possibly the only person in the UK for whom classical music, gaming shop ownership, internet cafes, and a volcano led to an eventual career in cybersecurity.

I grew up in Warwickshire, England in the seventies as the eldest child of Caribbean parents in those equality sections on forms, I identify myself as black-British (Caribbean). As you can probably imagine, I've always had to deal with race. Indeed, one of my earliest memories relates to discrimination based on the colour of my skin. I've experienced bullying at school and work, had obscenities yelled at me in the street, the beady eyes of shopkeepers following me as if I were going to steal something and being assertive resulted in being labelled as an 'aggressive black woman'. Being female doesn't give me a pass and in some ways, it can make things more difficult.

It's a commonly held belief in the Black and Asian Minority Ethnic (BAME) community in England that we must work twice as hard and be twice as good as a person with white skin. It's no surprise then that, during an upbringing that seemed strict compared to that of my white friends, my parents introduced the concept of working hard to achieve goals early on. One of the biggest moments for me was when I discovered classical music at the age of 11 and declared that I wanted a piano. My parents said that I could only have one if I passed the 12+ exam. This was a test that would determine which secondary school I would attend and, in doing so, help define who I am today. I passed the test and got my first piano!

Having achieved the goal of the piano and armed with the perfectionist's mantra "If I can't do it well, then I won't do it at all", I attended an all-girls grammar school whose Latin motto meant 'she sets heights in her heart'. We were encouraged to believe that we could do great things, and that being female shouldn't stand in our way. Two female teachers shared the tuition of computer studies. Male students travelled from a local boys' grammar school to study with our teachers - so it never occurred to me that computing wasn't something for girls. At the time, I didn't realise how fortunate I was to hold this view. It's only as I've looked back on my teenage years and education that I've really come to appreciate those two teachers as role models.

Alongside playing the piano, I became a computer gamer, way before it became a cool thing to do. My first experience of computer gaming was playing tennis on the TV in about 1981. My brother and I competed - moving the racquet lines up and down by turning a knob left or right and watching the square 'ball' travel between them, which kept us entertained for hours at a time.

A couple of years later I remember going to a computer store with mum, where we bought an Acorn Electron which had 32 kilobytes of memory and came with a bundle of 5 games on cassette tape. We'd take it in turns to play 'Snapper' and, thinking back on this now, I realise how lucky I was that my mum nurtured my interest in computing. I chose text-based adventure games where you could guide the direction of play and would happily spend ages carefully typing code from a magazine to play a game that was gone forever once you exited. As such, I learned basic coding skills early on.

I then progressed to the Archimedes 3000 with a whole 1 megabyte of memory; one of my friends had something called an Apple Mac and another had a BBC B Micro. We'd rotate houses and play the different games - this continued through much of my teens. It's amusing now to think that, despite the strict upbringing, my parents would let me have boys in my room because we were using the computer. In 'The Rise of the Cyber Women Volume 1' (p11), Lauren Zink wrote how her parents knew that taking away her keyboard was a real punishment. Thankfully, mine didn't. Although the keyboard was part of the computer on the A3000, so it would have meant taking the whole unit away!

However, this meant two keyboards were now vying for my attention. Even at this relatively early age, I suggested computerisation options whilst at my Work Experience placements; I was employed as a part-time pianist and music technician at college and coached students in the use of music notation software.

Given the subject of this book, you'd be forgiven for thinking that the computer keyboard won out over the piano when I started university. In fact, I studied classical music at Colchester Institute School of Music. My mum died the month before I started university. Despite, or perhaps because of this, I threw myself into university life. Within the first few months, I was elected Chair of the Students' Music Association – a role which involved planning and coordinating the committee to deliver various socials, balls, and concert trips within a small budget. I was also elected to represent my fellow students at course committee meetings.

During the Christmas break, I spent my savings on my first 'proper' PC - a Packard Bell with Windows 3.1 for Workgroups and an early iteration of Word and Excel. I didn't have internet access though; I had to go to the library or the sole PC in the music department for that.

By my second year, I had bought and hooked up a modem with dial-up connection at home, getting me 'online' with services such as Compuserve and AOL. I'd happily spend time chatting online with complete strangers, blissfully ignorant of modern concepts such as online safety. Of course, I had no idea about networking, only that configuring settings on my PC meant I could get online and collect my e-mail. So, when I entered those same settings into the computer in the music department and they didn't work, I was quite confused. I'd regularly report it to the IT guy, he'd come and fix it and the process would begin again. To this day, I think about how much work that technician could have saved himself by spending 5 minutes explaining to me what not to do and why – a lesson that I try to apply when coaching and training staff.

I excelled academically and, although shy, thrived socially during university; however, the study and extra-curricular activities became unbalanced in my final year. I was on course for a 1st class honours degree and graduated with a 2nd class with honours. This was a very harsh lesson for me. I felt as though I had let down all those who had supported me and most of all - myself. It still stings, acting as a constant reminder about the impact of over-committing myself.

In my final year at university (1997) my planned career as a musicologist specialising in black classical musicians took a bit of a twist and lot of a turn, when I decided to postpone doing a PhD to open a specialist computer game shop in my hometown. My motivation for the change? There was a cool computer game shop in Colchester and my hometown had nothing like it; the best it could muster up was a couple of shelves in Woolworths. So, in the Easter break, whilst others were sensibly finalising dissertations and studying for exams, I spent 3 1/2 days attending a Business Training Course through Enterprise Link. I finished my degree and started trading in July 1997.

As the sole proprietor, if I wanted something done, I had to either pay someone or learn to do it myself and, in most cases, it was the latter. I learned a huge amount, from negotiating with suppliers; balancing the books; to marketing and much more – all transferable skills that I would use as a manager in later life. A kind customer coded a simple website for me and learning how to edit the pages was my first experience of website development. I acquired a solid reputation for excellent customer service based upon honesty (another trait instilled in me at home), with customers coming in for impartial advice on games and the latest technologies. I added a fortnightly gaming club, and the shop became a friendly and safe place for gamers to hang out. It was a proud moment for me when a shy teenage girl told me she wanted to be like me when she grew up, with her own computer game shop. Word of mouth remained the most effective form of advertising and I broke even within six months.

Due to my school's positive attitude, the first time I remember feeling 'different' due to my gender rather than my race was when I attended an industry meeting of independent game shop owners. I sat to the left of the chairman and agreed to take notes for the meeting as he'd given me a lift there. The only woman around the table, everyone assumed I was his secretary and were stunned to find out I was a shop owner attending in my own right. The lesson for me (that I later forgot) was that if I wanted to be taken seriously, I shouldn't take notes at a meeting.

I was thrilled to get coverage from 'Indie', the trade magazine for independent game retailers, for the shop's first birthday - yet the interview reminded me how unusual I was. In the article the journalist starts by describing the typical male game store owner reading the magazine and how what they don't know about the games retail trade isn't worth knowing anyway before dropping this on them:

"Now consider, if you will, a different and somewhat unique perspective on the game, that of a recruit to the battle arena that is games retail. Not only a recruit, but one who considers the experience to be little more an exercise, an interesting project that has interrupted a grander, more glamorous plan. And get this, it's a woman, or more accurately, a girl. Surely some mistake that a woman should dare to treat this Y-chromosome-dominated marketplace as little more than a challenge. After all, this is the industry where women are more than welcome to muck in, as long as they don't mind handing out flyers at trade shows or using their feminine charms in a PR capacity." **(Dave McLean, Indie Magazine, August 1998)**

At cybersecurity conferences, 22 years later, we still see women dressed in scanty clothing handing out flyers to attract men to their exhibits. This does nothing to encourage more women into the field or reduce the abuse some women have experienced at these events - culminating in Jane Frankland's InSecurity Code of Conduct which conference organisers are encouraged to sign up to.

We also still see instances of female professionals working harder than their male counterparts in supposedly identical roles. Ironically, a data breach once bought this to my attention before the days of rules and transparency regarding gender pay disparity. A male colleague was found to be earning 25% more than my salary for the same job. I was shocked and upset enough to raise this with my boss, who increased my salary rather than arguing. Although I'd like to think this unfairness is a thing of the past, the IT and cybersecurity fields have a long way to go to achieve true equality. The more women who join us, the better. Fast forward to 2021 and I believe it is largely thanks to joining the computer gaming (and board gaming, to a lesser extent) community that I have the skills and traits to make me well suited to a career in Cybersecurity.

In turn-based strategy games such as 'Civilisation' I developed my spreadsheet skills in Excel to track information that wasn't otherwise available; figuring out the most efficient way of going about a task helped to develop my analytical skills. The gaming community developed an Excel spreadsheet to manage the city treasury in the massive multiplayer online roleplaying game (MMORPG) Star Wars Galaxies. I learned how to write formulas to tweak the tool to achieve what I needed. It's also the game in which I met my husband, but that's a whole other story!

In MMORPGs, I made new friends; joined 'guilds' (groups of like-minded players) and we'd go off on fantastical adventures in amazing digital worlds. These would typically require a group of players with different roles who would need to exercise their various skills to solve problems and puzzles; learning how to work together using one another's strengths to successfully achieve the objective. It's the perfect place to learn about teamwork and you don't succeed without attention to detail.

A certain type of gamer also demonstrates real tenacity, going to great lengths to solve these problems and puzzles. My strongly instilled sense of ethics around fairness might lead me to describe some of these means used as 'cheating'; the cybersecurity professional in me now recognises this as evidence of a 'hacking' mindset. The furthest I got into this was facilitating looking up cheat codes on the internet, which might give customers at my computer games store a sneaky advantage in their games. This later translated into a choice not to become a penetration tester – as, it is unnatural for me to look for ways to intentionally break things. Nevertheless, I consider tenacity in the face of adversity one of my strengths, and it is a quality that I look for when recruiting.

Devastatingly, my shop burned down in a fire, on Valentine's Day in 1999. I re-located and, after briefly considering working in web design, took a part-time position as Customer Service Assistant at the Internet Exchange, an Internet café. I became store manager and really enjoyed my time there as I was able to combine my love of this thing called the 'Internet' with the opportunity to help people learn how to use it, and computers more generally. My unit was the top of all stores across the country for a significant promotion in conjunction with a then little-known company called 'Amazon'. By the end of my time there I was manager of over 20 staff across three store units.

Thanks to the IT guy who setup the networked PCs, I also left knowing what IP addresses and subnets were, and finally understood why I couldn't get my e-mail on the music PC at university!

Having left the Internet Exchange for personal reasons, I invested in myself and took out a loan to fund a Computeach course on database design as it struck me that databases seemed a good way of organising information and I do like improving processes and systems. I then took an opportunity within the local council as a Help Desk Operator to get my foot in the door in an Information, Communications, and Technology Services ('ICT Services') department. My retail experience proved invaluable here, and I was able to improve the perception of ICT Services throughout the council by introducing a professional customer-focused approach to the Help Desk. The positive feedback from staff about my weekly Helpdesk Hints reminded me how much I'd enjoyed showing people how to do things at the Internet Exchange and, for a while, my professional development activities took me down the 'IT trainer' route.

Later, during the time of e-government, going paperless and doing more with less, I leapt at the opportunity to project manage the consolidation of three council ICT help desks into one virtual 'Help Desk'. Despite successfully delivering the project, my desire to move into IT project management wasn't supported by my employer at the time. Taking things into my own hands, I learned what I could by osmosis, bought the textbook and successfully self-studied for the Prince 2 Practitioner Foundation Exam - an entry level project management certification in the UK.

...king on a project management role for different council partnership, I gained practical ...perience of influencing without authority, which equipped me for future roles leading ...formation security programmes. I learned that the time I invested in listening to people, ...d the issues they felt existed, really paid off in bringing them with me on projects. I am ...oud of my work engaging members of the public as stakeholders on projects too; ...rticularly one very vocal naysayer who became the strongest advocate for a project they ...d originally resisted.

...y life and work were then rudely disrupted in 2010 by a diagnosis of an aggressive form of ...east cancer, six months into another project and just weeks before my wedding abroad. ...ne oncologist agreed for me to proceed with the wedding on the understanding that we ...ould postpone the honeymoon so I could have surgery. The wedding went ahead despite ...e attempts of Eyjafjallajökull's volcanic ash cloud stopping all flights across Europe!

...ad to take a year out for treatment including chemotherapy and significant surgeries. With ...e help of family, friends, and a new puppy, I finally recovered from these in February 2011.

...s a result of treatment, I have disabilities that are invisible to others, so, sometimes, it is ...ry tempting not to tick the box on applications forms. Nevertheless, I always do, because ...the UK equalities legislation exists to protect us. The box-ticking has given me the ...portunity to have open and frank conversations with my employers about the difficulties I ...ce in daily life and the reasonable adjustments I need to support me. I've had several ...ccupational health assessments and whilst, in my opinion, these exist to protect the ...ganisation more than the employees - it is fair to say that an employer would be wise to act ...n any reasonable adjustments they recommend. In this case, my employer handled my ...turn to work well and visited me at home to discuss my return. Feeling very apprehensive ...out it, I'd equipped myself with information from Macmillan Cancer Support and Breast ...ancer Care and drafted a schedule that I thought I could manage. My employer performed a ...sk assessment and implemented the reasonable adjustments.

...efore I knew it, I was right back into the swing of things although my mental faculties ...dn't feel as sharp as they used to. A former colleague once asked me "How do you know all ...is stuff?" after I'd delivered some information security training. There is a lot of ...formation to keep abreast of within cybersecurity and, whilst I never had a photographic ...emory, my recall ability was significantly reduced post chemotherapy treatment. I have ...veloped effective systems for myself to capture and retrieve information when I need it, ...cluding the mind mapping technique developed by Tony Buzan. I also read a lot of books ...d use the internet. We are so lucky these days with content creators freely sharing their ...nowledge on blogs, YouTube, and other services, not to mention massive open online ...urses (MOOCs). I would encourage anyone considering a career in such a constantly ...veloping industry to take full advantage of peer networks, mentoring, social media and ...her online professional communities and all the afore-mentioned shared knowledge.

...October, my husband and I found out that, due to the cancer treatment, I wouldn't be able ...have children. This news was followed by another surgery and a month off work. On my ...turn, I knew I was ready for a change – I just wasn't quite sure what.

In 2012, a dull-sounding data classification role was re-pitched to me as 'how we use and protect people's information'. Despite my relative lack of experience, the person making the pitch said they were willing to take a risk on me if I was willing to take a risk too. I was, and I did. So began my career as a cybersecurity professional and a huge learning curve, which I relished. I consider myself fortunate that there were two men, in other roles at that organisation, who understood that I didn't have an information security background and were keen to support me in my learning.

The more I learned, the more it struck me just how oblivious most people were (and still are) to the value of their information and the need to protect it. I noticed through my learning online that, unlike in retail or IT, it appeared to be common for cybersecurity professionals to include post-nominals on their profiles indicating that they had completed academic and/or professional certifications. I researched which ones were associated with managing information security programmes and chose to self-study for the ISACA Certified Information Security Manager exam; this provided me with a solid grounding on which to build.

Over three years, the role expanded into my becoming the senior professional subject matter expert with corporate responsibility for information security, data protection, open data and transparency, information management, records, and document management. Whilst I enjoyed the variety of the role, I was dissatisfied spreading myself so thinly across each discipline; I wanted to delve deeper. I was most interested in learning more about information security, so I decided to start looking for a new job with a narrower scope. At that point I didn't realise just how broad and deep the field of information security was and how different industry sectors have slightly different challenges.

I created a skills inventory for myself and identified practical examples from my life to demonstrate how I'd approached and dealt with each one, using the STAR technique (situation - task - action - result). This triggered forgotten memories and opened my eyes to how well suited I was for some jobs.[7] It taught me that we should apply for roles that appeal to us even if we don't think we meet all their requirements. We may be pleasantly surprised; particularly as I've found that some organisations don't know what they need from a cybersecurity professional. Adverts looking for the 'unicorn' cybersecurity professional don't help those of us that suffer from 'Imposter Syndrome' which is very common amongst both women and men in our industry. Amy Ertan wrote in vol 1 (p185) that 'the more underrepresented you are, the more you are likely to feel self-doubt'. As you've seen, I check several minority boxes. I wish I could disagree with Amy's statement, but for me it's been all too true. Unfortunately, for me, other traits have proved more difficult to handle within my profession. I suffer with perfectionism[8] and am a 'Complete Finisher'[9], making it difficult for

---

[7] I learnt most of my interview techniques, both as interviewee and interviewer, from the 'Manager Tools' podcast (see https://www.manager-tools.com/map-universe/being-interviewed). I also recommend reading 'The Effective Hiring Manager' (Horstman, 2020).

[8] There are three key elements to perfectionism that transform it from being a positive into a negative:
1. The relentless striving for extremely high standards (for yourself and/or others) that are personally demanding, in the context of the individual. (Typically, to an outsider the standards are considered to be unreasonable given the circumstances.)

me to accept that tasks I've committed to might not get done. In the last 12 months at work, I ran from meeting to meeting and completed tasks outside of work hours every day. I let three or four hours of sleep each night become the norm and would sometimes work through the night to get things done. Despite my husband and friends telling me, I didn't realise the damage I was doing to myself. My advice is to never ever do this. It's not good for you, it's not good for your relationships and it's not good for your organisation. As a former colleague recently said to me, "No job is worth it; no matter how great the cause." For me, this approach led to burnout.

Although I acknowledge that my burnout is due in part to some of my personal traits, it's important to be honest about the pressures of an unrelenting industry. The work of cybersecurity will never be 'done'. Every day cyber-criminals are responsible for another data breach, developers for another vulnerability, a department head for a major procurement they didn't follow process for, and so it goes on.

Whether it's exercise, reading, gaming, cognitive behavioural therapy (CBT) or something else, it's important to give ourselves downtime and find sustainable ways to relax and decompress. I'm pleased to see, through webinars and social media conversations, that the industry recognises the importance of good mental health and resilience.

The lesson for me is to always look after my health first, ditch my perfectionist's mantra and to try and live by a new one to

"Do the best I can in the time available and trust that it'll be good enough."

As I hope I've shown through my career journey, everyone's path into cybersecurity is different. Each of us carries with us a wealth of life experience that has equipped us with the skills we need to excel in this vibrant field – however weird and wonderful that experience might be. Ever-changing, reflective yet forward-facing, cybersecurity allows us the opportunity to build on, or discard, parts of this experience and constantly regenerate – whether at an individual, organisational or system-wide level. So, we can have heights set in our hearts and a realistic chance of achieving them. By embracing and encouraging varied CVs, approach routes and passions, cybersecurity also has the potential to value diversity, encourage compassion and be truly inclusive. Who wouldn't want a career in an industry like that?

If you do and are wondering where to start, my top recommendations are to (i) read Jessica Barker's excellent introductory book[10], (ii) learn about the different types of job roles[11] and

---

2. Judging your self-worth based largely on your ability to strive for and achieve such unrelenting standards.
3. Experiencing negative consequences of setting such demanding standards yet continuing to go for them despite the huge cost to you.

Source: Centre for Clinical Interventions Perfectionism in perspective workbook
https://www.cci.health.wa.gov.au/Resources/Looking-After-Yourself/Perfectionism

[9] 'Complete Finisher' is one of nine team roles as defined by Dr Meredith, see
https://www.belbin.com/about/belbin-team-roles/

[10] "Confident Cyber Security How to Get Started in Cyber Security and Futureproof Your Career" (Barker, Kogan Page,2020) I have written a review on Goodreads that explains why I recommend it:
https://www.goodreads.com/review/show/3550698487?book_show_action=true&from_review_page=1

(iii) find a mentor[12].

---

[11] Whilst cybersecurity may seem niche, it's actually very broad with a sub-discipline to suit people with different backgrounds and skillsets. My favourite resource for this is the NICE Cybersecurity Workforce Framework (https://niccs.cisa.gov/workforce-development/cyber-security-workforce-framework) which defines 52 roles across 33 specialty areas grouped into 7 common functions. Much like the IT focused SFIAplus (a version of the Skills for the Information Age (SFIA) framework that is available to BCS members), it deconstructs the roles into Skills, Knowledge, Abilities and Tasks and you can search on these to help identify potential roles for you.
Although it is US based, it is far more comprehensive than the UK based CIISec Capability Development Methodology (https://www.ciisec.org/Capability_Methodology) which at this time contains just 11 roles mapped to their skills and knowledge frameworks.
Another good source is the careers section of the Cyber Security Challenge UK website (https://www.cybersecuritychallenge.org.uk/resources/careers).

[12] There are several mentoring schemes run by professional bodies such as ISACA London, as well as some from other organisations and communities such as Cybersecurity Mentoring Hub (https://cybersecmentorship.org). Other approaches include putting out a call on twitter on a Monday using the hashtag #cybermentoringmonday or reaching out to people in your professional network.

Coming in March 2022 - The Rise of the Cyber Women: Volume 3

"The Rise of the Cyber Women: Volume 3" will be a compilation of inspiring stories and accounts from women in the cyber security and technology industries who are pioneers and leading the way in helping to protect the world from the growing cyber threat. It is hoped that this book will feature men in the cyber security industry from all over the world.

Those who are included and featured in the book will give their hints, tips, and advice to those who are looking to pursue a career in cyber security or technology or change their career path into cyber security or technology.

Submission Requirements

The Editor is looking for inspirational stories and accounts from women in the cyber security industry from all over the world who would like to be featured in the book, which will be released via Amazon Kindle Direct Publishing.

We are ideally looking to feature:

- Women who haven't had a linear path or journey into the cyber security and technology industries.
- Women who entered the cyber security and technology industries from a non-technical background.
- Women who started out in an entirely different industry to cyber security and technology.
- Women who have overcome challenges or adversary to get to where they are today in cyber security or technology.

We would love chapters to contain any relevant inspirational quotes, hints, and tips that you have which will encourage other women to enter the industry. And if you have had any animosity from any of your colleagues, male or female, we'd also love to know how you dealt with this.

We look forward to receiving your chapter submissions for volume three of "The Rise of the Cyber Women: Volume 3".

Made in the USA
Monee, IL
08 March 2021